ALFRED DEN

SOCRATES

AND ATHENIAN SOCIETY IN HIS DAY

A BIOGRAPHICAL SKETCH

Elibron Classics
www.elibron.com

SOCRATES

SOCRATES

AND ATHENIAN SOCIETY IN HIS DAY

A BIOGRAPHICAL SKETCH

BY

A. D. GODLEY, M.A.

Fellow of Magdalen College, Oxford

LONDON
SEELEY AND CO. LIMITED
ESSEX STREET, STRAND

1896

PREFACE

THIS work is not intended for classical scholars or professed Platonists; but rather for the large and increasing class of students who do not wish to be debarred altogether from an acquaintance with Greek literature by their ignorance of the Greek language. For the benefit of such readers I have endeavoured, with the help of extracts selected mostly from Plato, to draw a picture of Socrates' relation to his immediate *entourage* and to Athenian society in general. This being the object in view, the passages chosen—except indeed the myths, which whether strictly "Socratic" or not, are sometimes the most important part of a Socratic dialogue—are generally such as bear comparatively little reference to the speculative and dogmatic sides of Socrates' teaching, while on the other hand they tend to throw light on his habits and character, and the way in which he was regarded by his contemporaries. But it is especially difficult in this case to separate the philosopher from the man.

CONTENTS

SOCRATES

CHAPTER I

ATHENS BEFORE AND AFTER THE PERSIAN WARS

THE all-important era in the history of Athens was the Persian War, and the victories of Marathon and Salamis; before the opening of the fifth century B.C. neither town nor people was in any way markedly differentiated from the rest of the little self-centred communities of Greece. Perhaps there are here and there indications of a quicker and brighter intelligence, a more restless spirit of enterprise. Herodotus cites Athenians as being distinguished for their "social gift" and conversational powers; and the fame of Solon, and later of Cleisthenes, is pre-eminent among early Greek legislators. They enjoyed, too, the nearly unique distinction in history of being, as Athenian speakers

B

remind the rest of Greece, αὐτόχθονες,—descendants, that is, of the "original" inhabitants of
Attica. Separated by natural boundaries from
Peloponnesus, and dwelling (as a glance at the map
will show) outside the paths which would naturally
be followed by the half-mythical, half-historical
"Dorian invasion" which had submerged the old
Achaian civilisation of Homeric times beneath
an influx of hard-fighting but comparatively bar-
barous northerners, Attica had retained the old
Ionic population, and the old Ionic speech practically unchanged. The race which was to colonise
and subdue the valley of the Eurotas pressed
southwards over the Corinthian isthmus, and left
the Athenians dwelling between the mountains and
the Aegean Sea—partly, as I have said, because
they lay outside the path of the invader ; and partly,
no doubt, because Peloponnesus offered a fairer
spoil than the comparatively unproductive plain
of Attica. The history of the "Eye of Greece"
had in fact been singularly unchequered till the
latter part of the sixth century. Her mythical
renown is indebted for its principal lustre to the
adornments added, as was natural, by the art of
dramatist and sculptor. Her political history,
until the expulsion of the Pisistratid family and

the legislation of Cleisthenes, does not widely differentiate her from the rest of Hellas. And of the later splendour of Athenian architecture there was, at the end of the sixth century, as little trace as there was any sign of the development of the Euripidean drama. The town was still "that little earlier Athens of Peisistratus which the Persians destroyed, which some of us " (so wrote Mr. Pater in his *Greek Studies*) "perhaps would rather have seen, in its early simplicity, than the greater one : . . . its little buildings on the hill-top, still with steep rocky ways, crowding round the ancient temple of Erechtheus and the grave of Cecrops, with the old miraculous olive tree still growing there, and the old snake of Athene Polias still alive somewhere in the temple court."

It was the Athenians who were the heroes of the Persian War, and they were also its immediate cause. That spirit of enterprise, which then and afterwards was her characteristic, had prompted Athens to assist the Asiatic Greeks in their revolt against the Great King ; and an Athenian force accompanied the Ionians to the destruction of Sardis, the Persian capital of Western Asia Minor. With the ostensible object of punishing the Athenians, Darius despatched more than one

expedition against the Greek coasts: his lieu-
tenants, Datis and Artaphernes, succeeded in
landing at Marathon in Attica, but were driven
back to their ships with great slaughter by an
Athenian force. Ten years later (in 480 B.C.)
Darius' son and successor Xerxes led into Greece
a mixed multitude collected from the various
quarters of the huge Persian "empire." Once
more his principal or at least his alleged aim
was vengeance on the now doubly guilty Athenians ; and in so far as concerned the material
structure of the Athenian city, vengeance was
complete enough. Athens, for the moment, was
obliterated from the map of Greece. But her
citizens had taken refuge either in neighbouring
towns or in the powerful fleet which had been con-
structed under the auspices of their statesman and
general Themistocles. Hardly had the smoke of
the burning city ceased to go up, when the monster
armament of Xerxes was confronted by Athens
and the allied contingents of Hellas in the famous
strait of Salamis ; in a few hours Xerxes' admirals
were swept from the Greek waters, and the danger
of a Persian naval invasion was for ever at an end.
In the next year the victory of Plataea saved
Greece once for all from fear of Oriental dominion

All through this desperate struggle Athens stands out prominently as the leader of Greece. It was she, and she alone, who conquered at Marathon : it was her fleet that assured the victory at Salamis.

Writing about half-a-century later, Herodotus assigns the glory of the Persian repulse to the constancy and forethought and decision of men who had made up their minds to entertain no thought of truce with the invader. "It is not," he says, "too much to call them saviours of Hellas, for whichever side they took, victory must needs follow them." The Spartans no doubt were as brave, but they lacked the swiftness and adaptability of the Athenian. Thus it was that, as Plato writes in the *Timaeus* of the legendary glories of a mythic Athens, the city "shone conspicuous in the sight of all men for valour and might ; foremost in courage and the arts of war, now in the van of the armies of Hellas, now forced by desertion to stand alone, she shrank from no hazard, however desperate ; vanquished the invader, and set up trophies of victory."

The old Athens was gone. But a new and a greater Athens arose from its ashes. The city was now for the first time fortified, and, what was

still more important, walls were built to protect
the communication with her port, Piraeus, as
became a State that aimed at maritime dominion,
and the recognised leader of the great anti-Persian
alliance. For the first and almost the only time
in history, a maritime Panhellenic confederacy
was now organised, to protect Hellas against the
possibility of another attack from the East. In
this confederacy the Athenians were at first only
primi inter pares. Its centre was originally not
Athens but Delos ; each State was to supply a
stated number of ships and men, and it was left
to Athens to utilise these supplies against the
common enemy to the best advantage. But, as
was to be expected, primacy grew into dominion ;
the leader became a ruler. Many causes con-
tributed to this result ; notably the fact that in a
majority of cases the troublesome contribution of
ships and men was commuted for a money pay-
ment into the common treasury at Delos, a com-
mutation which enriched the fund while at the
same time weakening the actual fighting-power
of the contributing State. In course of time this
treasure was transferred—apparently by common
consent, and not by any high-handed action on
the part of Athens—from Delos to the Acropolis;

and this may be said to mark the foundation of
the Athenian empire. Athens thus became no
longer the head of a federation, but an imperial
city receiving, and in case of necessity exacting,
an annual tribute from subject communities. Nor
was the growth of Athens slower on the mainland
of Hellas. Her naval supremacy, bringing with it
an increased development of her commercial relations, as well as the actual wealth derived from the
tribute paid to her, enabled her to lay the foundations of empire near home by practically annexing
Boeotia and Megara.

About or shortly after the middle of the fifth
century, hardly any scheme of ambition could
seem impossible to an Athenian. The Aegean
was practically "an Athenian lake"; Boeotia, if
not actually subject, was in the hands of an "Atti-
cising" democracy; while the control of Megara
and the adjoining district meant the command of
the land communication with the Peloponnesus—
for the difficult pass between the heights of Mount
Geraneia and the sea could easily be held by a hand-
ful of resolute men who were in possession of the
Megarid. But the tide soon began to turn. Both
Megara and Boeotia revolted ; a decisive battle
almost annihilated an Athenian force and restored

the exiled Theban oligarchies, and the loss of the isthmus of Corinth exposed Attica once more to invasion from the Peloponnesus. All hope of an empire on the mainland was once for all swept away. Athens concluded the celebrated Thirty Years' Truce in 445 B.C., on terms which three years before she would never have dreamt of accepting.

Such, in a few words, is the history of Athens' successes and failures outside her borders up to 445 B.C. Her internal history also is one of rapid and complete change, material and social.

The architectural development of Athens itself testifies to her increasing wealth and resources. The city itself had been fortified shortly after Salamis; twenty years later it was connected by long walls with the port of Piraeus, and the new town which grew up round the harbour was rebuilt and laid out in straight streets. Thus the Athenians assured their communications with the sea; they were no longer dwellers in a mere hill-fort, but citizens of a maritime city. On and round the Acropolis sprang up the beautiful buildings which still in great part exist; all these, however, belong to the period when Athens had passed her prime of success; the Parthenon, Propylaea, and Odeon were not commenced till after the conclusion of the Thirty Years' Truce. Two great names are associated with their construction—the names of Pericles and Phidias. The former for the last twenty years of his life had controlled Athens and Athenian development in almost every direction. His ideal was not the concord of Hellas, but the pre-eminence of Athens alone ; she was to be first in Hellas as he was first in Athens, and to this end probably as much as any other, he lavished the public money and employed the first sculptor of the age in so adorning the city of which he was the practical sovereign, that her magnificence should impress all beholders with the conviction of her wealth and power. More especially the majestic edifices of the Acropolis would form the most effective contrast to the humble, unpretending streets of Sparta, which seems never—even at the zenith of Laconian greatness—to have advanced beyond the condition of a mere mountain village.

The reforms introduced into the Athenian constitution by Cleisthenes were the foundation but not the full development of democracy. But the victory of Salamis had been won, although under the leadership of great and ancient families, yet by the sinew and the valour of the commonalty ;

and it was only natural that when the "sailor populace" came back to its home it should claim a larger share in the government of the city. Through the changes introduced by various statesmen—and with these changes the name of Pericles himself is prominently connected—the Athenian constitution became the most completely democratic that the world has yet seen. To the people themselves, assembled *en masse* in the Ecclesia, questions of foreign and domestic policy were referred ; cases in the law-courts were decided, not by small juries or single experts, but by large bodies of citizens. Thus the whole body of the Athenian people came to be composed of lawyers and politicians : little or nothing was delegated to representatives ; Demos decided for himself,—having plenty of time, as he employed slave labour. It was inevitable that this continual occupation in the business of the bar and the State should have the greatest educational influence ; for good or bad the popular intelligence was bound to develop ; and when we remember also that the position of Athens placed her in constant intercourse with all sorts and conditions of foreigners, and that her wealth and her political importance made her a "literary and artistic centre," where, at any rate after the close of the first half of the fifth century, every citizen was privileged to see and hear all that was best in art and literature (that is, the drama), and to watch the earliest efforts of that contemporary intellectual development which remains the wonder of the world—recalling this, we shall not be surprised at the difference between the public of Socrates' middle life and the men who fought at Marathon. Aristophanes is never tired of insisting on the difference between the simple-minded, hard-headed, and hard-fisted "warriors of Marathon, sturdy old hearts of oak," and their sons or grandsons, with their eager inquisitiveness, their irreverence for antiquity, their sceptical spirit of discussion. The day of the old fighting-man is now over. Poor old dotard! he has lived too long, into an age that knows him not; all his exploits are forgotten, and he is badgered by young advocates in the law-courts; where of course he loses his case and goes home whimpering to his friends οὗ μ' ἐχρῆν σορὸν πρίασθαι τοῦτ' ὀφλὼν ἀπέρχομαι: "I am mulcted by the court of the sum that should have bought my coffin!"

Thus in every direction, internally as well as externally, the development of Athens had been

rapid and startling. Even after the conclusion
of the Thirty Years' Truce she was undoubtedly
the first city of Hellas; but she had not achieved
her greatness without incurring inevitable jealousy
and hatred. Perhaps the Athenian name was
never really popular in Greece, except immediately
after the close of the Persian wars, when all her
fellow communities were dazzled by the glamour
of her brilliant heroism and brilliant success.
Every other feeling was overcome for the moment
by the gratitude felt towards the State which
had freed all Greece from the common danger;
but a pre-eminence built upon gratitude is of no
long duration. Fifty years afterwards Herodotus
is obliged to apologise for his conviction that
Athens was the saviour of Hellas: " I make this
statement," he says, " though I am aware that it
will be displeasing to most men." Fear of Athenian
activity obliterated remembrance of Athenian past
services. Boeotia was her mortal enemy, Corinth a
maritime rival. More especially Sparta, once the
acknowledged head of Greece, must necessarily view
the rise of a rival with hardly-concealed jealousy.
That strange, self-contained community of fighting-
men, separated from the rest of Hellas no less by
the physical barrier of a high mountain chain

than by its peculiar and especially un-Attic life
and training, had originally held an acknowledged
position of supremacy in virtue of the iron
immutability of the Spartan constitution and
the lion-like courage of Spartan warriors—a position from which it was now deposed. Even a
Panhellenic confederacy with Sparta taking only
the second place would have been an outrage
to her feelings; and the object of Pericles and
his school was no Panhellenic confederacy, but
rather an Athenian empire. The "yoke-fellow of
Athens," as Sparta was called in the days when
the co-existence of two great states in Hellas was
still thought possible, was not unnaturally alarmed
by the extension of her rival's supremacy. At all
periods from Salamis onwards to 445 B.C., her
jealous alarm was shown in various ways. Sometimes Athens was actually at war with Sparta.
More often Laconian feeling was rather exhibited
by an undissembled sympathy with the enemies
and revolted subjects of the Athenians; and the
revolters had in most cases an especial claim to
such sympathy from the fact of their being
Dorians oppressed by Ionians. Relations between
the two States were always strained. When the
Peloponnesian War broke out in 431 B.C., fourteen

years after the conclusion of the truce, its causes
were ostensibly certain unimportant squabbles
between cities and colonists : in reality the *casus
belli* is to be found in the implacable animosity
between two States differing widely in race, habits,
and ideals—two States, moreover, which could not
be simultaneously great, the rise of the one involving the fall of the other.

In Plato's well-known story of the isle Atlantis,
a pre-historic Athens is represented as repelling
the forces of the island State, just as the later
Athenians defeated the Persians at Marathon and
Salamis.   The tale is related by a young Athenian
to Socrates at a festival.

THE STORY OF ATHENS AND ATLANTIS.

"Listen then, Socrates, to a story very strange
but altogether true, as Solon the wisest of the
Seven once said.   He was a connection and very
great friend of Dropidas our great-grandfather, as
he says himself in many passages of his poems :
and he told our grandfather Critias, as the old
man in turn repeated to us, that this city had of
old performed certain great and marvellous feats,

now forgotten by reason of the lapse of time and
the perishing of men : one amongst them greatest
of all, by relating which we shall both fittingly
pay our debt of gratitude to you and celebrate
the goddess at this festival justly and truly, as it
were with a hymn of praise."

"You say well. But what was this achievement
which, as Critias stated on Solon's authority, was
unrecorded but had really been performed by this
city in antiquity ? "

" I will tell you : the story is old, nor was he from
whom I heard it young. Critias had then, by his
own account, attained nearly to the age of ninety,
while I was about ten years old. It was that
day of the Apaturia which we call the Day of
Youth ; and we boys—according to the common
custom of the festival—were contending for prizes
of minstrelsy offered by our fathers. Among the
many works of many poets which were repeated,
not a few of us boys chose for recitation the
poems of Solon, as they were at that time new.
Now one of my kinsmen, whether speaking his
real mind or wishing to please Critias, said that
in his opinion Solon was as pre-eminently noble
a poet as he was pre-eminently wise in other
respects ; at which old Critias, as I well remember,

was much pleased, and said with a smile: 'Yes, Amynandrus; had Solon done like others and made poetry the business not only of his leisure but of his life, had he completed the story which he brought hither from Egypt, and not been compelled to neglect it by those civil discords and many mischiefs which he found at home on his return, to my thinking he would not have yielded the palm of honour to Hesiod or Homer or any other poet.' 'What then, Critias,' Amynandrus asked, 'was this tale?' 'It was the story,' said he, 'of what should be the most famous, as it was the greatest, of all achievements: one which, though the tradition of it has been interrupted by lapse of time and the passing away of its author, was indeed performed by this city.' 'Begin,' replied Amynandrus, 'at the beginning and tell me what the story was, and how Solon heard it, and who assured him of its truth.'

"'You must know then,' he said, 'that in the Delta of Egypt, the upper angle of which parts the waters of the Nile, there is a province called the Saitic, and the capital of this province is the town of Sais, the native place of King Amasis. This city is presided over by a goddess called in the Egyptian tongue Neith, and in Greek—

according to the statement of the inhabitants—
Athena ; and the people are very friendly to
Athens, and claim a sort of kinship with us.
Solon (such was his story) travelled to this place,
and was received there with great honour, and by
addressing the most learned of the priests and
questioning them on antiquities he became convinced that he and all the other Greeks were (if
we may say so) completely ignorant of these
matters. Once, wishing to lead the priests on to
speak of old times, he essayed to tell them our
own most ancient legends,—the story of Phoroneus,
the traditional first man, and Niobe ; then how
Deucalion and Pyrrha survived after the Deluge ;
and he traced the history of their descendants, and
tried to make a computation for his hearers of the
years which had elapsed by marking them off into
the different periods. Then said one of the priests,
a man of great age : " Solon, Solon, you Greeks are
ever children,—there are no old men in Hellas."
" How mean you by that ? " said Solon. " In soul,"
replied the priest, " you are all young ; for there you
have no ancient belief grounded on past tradition,
nor any lore of hoary antiquity. And the reason
of it is this :—Mankind has often been swept away
by various agencies : the most potent destroyers

have been fire and water, but countless other causes
have brought about a less complete destruction.
Even with you there is a tradition, that once upon
a time Phaethon the son of Helios harnessed
his father's horses, and being unable to drive the
chariot along his father's road consumed all that
was on the earth by fire, and was himself slain
by a thunderbolt: this tradition really describes
in the form of a legend that declension to which all
things that move on earth and in heaven are liable,
and those great conflagrations which at rare intervals periodically destroy the inhabitants of earth.

"'"At these times the dwellers in high and arid
lands are more exposed to destruction than those
who live by seas and rivers: as for us, the Nile
is as ever our constant protector, and saves us
from the difficulty by the release of his springs.
On the other hand, when the gods send a deluge
of water to purify the earth, the shepherds and
herdsmen in the mountains remain safe, but the
inhabitants of your cities are swept by the rivers
into the sea; while in this country there are no
descending streams then more than at other times
to overflow the fields ; on the contrary, all the
water naturally comes up from below.   Thus, and
for these reasons, the traditions here preserved are

the oldest that are recorded. The truth of the matter is this :—Every country not rendered inaccessible by excessive cold or heat is inhabited by some race of men periodically varying in numbers. With us, all deeds great or noble or in any way remarkable, whether they be done in your country or ours, or any known to us by hearsay, have been from remote antiquity enshrined here in a written record preserved in our temples. But no sooner have the records kept by you and the rest of the world been from time to time committed to writing and provided with the due equipment of State archives, than the customary period arrives when, like a pestilence, the deluge sweeps down upon them and leaves none of you but the unlearned and ignorant ; so that you begin afresh as it were a new life, knowing nothing about the ancient history of your own country or ours. You, Solon, are an instance of this : your genealogical chronicle of what has happened in Hellas is hardly better than a childish fable. To begin with, you Greeks can only remember the last of the many deluges, and moreover you are ignorant that your country was the birthplace of the fairest and best race in the world, a race of which the small remnant was the stock from which

you, Solon, and all your countrymen are descended.
All this you have forgotten, because many genera-
tions of the survivors lived and died without the
power of expressing themselves in writing.

"'" For long ago, before that great destroying
flood, the State now called Athenian was beyond all
others warlike, and in every respect pre-eminently
well governed. No city performed nobler acts than
she, and the forms of her constitution were the
fairest of all that hearsay has made known to us
under heaven." At this Solon, as he told me, was
astonished, and earnestly entreated the priests to
give him a full and exact account of the ancient
condition of his country. "Most willingly, Solon,"
replied the priest ; "I will do as you request not
only for your and your city's sake, but especially
as an act of gratitude to that goddess who received
your State and ours as her allotted share, and gave
nurture and education to your countrymen, whose
seed was delivered to her by Earth and Fire a
thousand years earlier than to ours. Now our
constitution—according to the computation of our
sacred books—has subsisted for 8,000 years, and
thus it was 9,000 years ago that your State first
came into being. Of that State's laws and its
one fairest achievement I will now give you a

brief account : presently we will consult the books
themselves, and examine at leisure the exact details
of your history in due order. For your laws, I
will refer you to our own ; for you will find many
among us now that are modelled on your ancient
institutions. You will see that the class of priests is
separate from the rest of the nation, and that the
artificers are likewise divided, each guild, whether
it be of shepherds or huntsmen or field-labourers,
pursuing its calling without intercourse with any
other. Moreover, you will probably have perceived
that the class of warriors is here distinct from all
the others, they being legally enjoined to occupy
themselves with war and nothing else. Then
again, they are armed with shield and spear—
a fashion of armour which was used by no
Asiatics before ourselves, and which the goddess
taught to you first as afterwards to Eastern nations.
In education, again, you see how careful our
law has been throughout to investigate the principles of the universe, even to the study of divination and the healing of diseases, and has turned
these divine influences to human use, and mastered
the branches of learning that naturally follow from
such principles.

   " ' " As ours is now, so was your State first marshalled and ordered by the goddess when she gave

you a place to dwell in, judging from the tempered clemency of its seasons that no place would be the mother of wiser men.

" ' " Being, then, a lover of war and of wisdom, the goddess selected and peopled that place which would produce a stock likest to herself; and so you who dwelt there enjoyed laws similar to, and even better than, ours, and your pre-eminence in every kind of excellence was such as befitted your divine origin and upbringing. Now among the many great deeds of your city which are here recorded for our wonder, there is one of surpassing magnitude and excellence. The books tell how once that city crushed a mighty host of invaders who came in upon us from the Atlantic Sea, and menaced in their pride Europe and Asia alike. For that sea was then navigable, as there was an island in it facing the passage which you call, as you say, the Pillars of Hercules, and this island was greater than Libya and Asia together. From it the travellers of that day could pass to the other islands, and from them to the whole extent of mainland which confronted them and bounded what was a sea in very truth (for all the waters within the passage which I have mentioned are like a lake with a narrow entrance; but the farther waters and the shores which enclose them may with the fullest truth and justice be termed open sea and mainland). So then in this isle of Atlantis there had grown up a mighty and marvellous royal dynasty, and it held sway over all the island, and many others besides, and parts of the continent. Moreover, they ruled even these nearer lands of ours, Libya as far as Egypt, and Europe to the confines of Italy. The united forces of their empire essaying to enslave at one blow your country and ours, and all the regions within the Straits,—then it was, Solon, that your State shone conspicuous in the sight of all men for valour and might : foremost in courage and the arts of war, now in the van of the armies of Hellas, now forced by desertion to stand alone, she shrank from no hazard however desperate; vanquished the invader, and set up trophies of victory ; saved those that were yet free from slavery, and to all the subject nations among us who dwell within the Heraclean boundary, gave generously the boon of freedom. But at a later day there came violent earthquakes and deluges; whereby, in one terrible day and night, all your fighting men were at once swallowed up by the earth, and in like manner the isle Atlantis was engulfed beneath the waves ; so that now the waters of that sea are impassable and unexplored, by reason of the very deep mud cast up by the sinking of the island." ' "

CHAPTER II

SOCRATES lived through the rapid transitions and fiery activities of the fifth century. Born in 469, he died in 399 B.C.; and thus his life really covers the whole period of Athenian greatness. He forms a link between the old Athens and the new. At his birth, it was still the city of the men who fought at Marathon. His prime of life coincides with the Periclean supremacy, and the beginning of the Peloponnesian War; and his teaching was carried on all through that terrible struggle. But as the literature associated with his name only here and there condescends to glance at contemporary history, so if we look for the name of Socrates in the annals of the time we are disappointed. He did his duty as a citizen and a soldier. He is recorded as serving in the army on two occasions; twice again he appears with some prominence as a juryman and a voter; but his

24

name is practically unknown to the political and military history of the period. To us at least he has nothing to do with all that; it is only when we come to the closing scene—to his trial and death—that the figure of Socrates is conspicuous in the theatre of contemporary events. The facts —so-called—of his life as narrated by Diogenes Laertius at a distance of several centuries, and the recollections of his pupil Xenophon, make up the chronicle of an uneventful life.

From the miscellaneous rubbish-heap which forms one of Diogenes Laertius' *Lives of the Philosophers*, it is to be gathered that Socrates was the son of Sophroniscus, a stone-mason; and that he may possibly have worked at the trade himself. According to one tradition, the Crito of Plato's dialogues, a coeval of Socrates, and belonging to the same deme (or, as we should say, the same parish), was responsible for the philosopher's education; but this, like most of the scanty information which we possess as to Socrates' early life, is at least exceedingly doubtful. Most of Diogenes' anecdotes are intended to illustrate the unconventional simplicity of Socrates' mode of living; and herein Diogenes does not add very much to Xenophon, on whom he draws largely throughout.

From Socrates' own statement it is known that
he never left Athens, except on military duty—in
this respect unlike the majority of professional
teachers, who journeyed from place to place, now
lecturing in Athens, now in Syracuse—wherever
there was likely to be a market for their wares.
He served in the army during the Peloponnesian War, being then a man of mature age ;
Alcibiades, in Plato's *Banquet*, draws a glowing
picture of his courage and endurance in the
campaign of Potidaea, and his presence of mind
in the rout of the Athenian force at Delium ; and
he was also in the army at Amphipolis. Probably
by this time he would be a sufficiently well-known
figure in the Athenian streets—at least in a town
where every one was known by sight, the remarkable ugliness which Socrates himself describes in
Xenophon's version of the *Banquet* (and which
certainly appears in the portrait transmitted to
our time), coupled with his peculiarly and almost
ostentatiously simple habit of life, would, even
apart from his reputation as a controversialist of
the streets, have made him familiar to the general
eye. But as a public man he was not known.
He was no politician ; indeed it is hard to see
what sympathy the philosopher could have had

with the plots and squabbles and litigations which
Athens dignified by the name of politics; how he
could have failed to despise a populace as fickle
and passionate at home as short-sighted and
selfish abroad; wholly destitute of any conception
of political stability; foolishly proud of its freedom, yet the dupe and the slave of the latest
demagogue. In such a State, Socrates could
hardly have wished to do more than "jouk and
let the jaw go by." Such in effect is the advice
given by Plato to the wise man fallen on evil
days. He was, as he says in his *Defence*, un-
practised in the ways of litigation: "This is
my first appearance in a court of law" (that is,
as a party in a case) "for all my seventy years."
On two occasions, however, he comes into prominence in connection with matters of public
interest. After the naval defeat of the Athenians
off Arginusae in the year 406 B.C. public indignation
at Athens ran high against the admirals of the
fleet, who had been in such a hurry to quit the
scene of the disaster that they had neglected to
pick up the bodies of their slain comrades; and
the general cry was for a condemnation *en bloc*.
Socrates, who was then one of the "prytanes" or
temporary presidents of the Council (βουλή)

refused to allow this proposal to be put to the vote, although his opposition came near to costing him his life. Again, he was ordered by the "Thirty Tyrants" to arrest one of their enemies, a certain Leon, with a view to his execution: this Socrates refused to do, and was nearly put to death for his independence. He was saved by the fall of the Thirty.

Withal, Socrates was a personage in Athens; and his very non-interference in politics must have made him an object of suspicion and fear to a government conscious of its own defects and weakness, and all the more sensitive to the criticism of contemptuous indifference. Socrates' attitude was in some respects like that of the Roman Stoics in the first century of the Empire: their opposition, like his, consisted rather in silence than in outspoken disapproval; just as a Thrasea or a Helvidius was challenged in the Senate rather to speak his mind openly than to insult the government by a morose policy of non-intervention, so one may well imagine that "practical politicians" might have called on Socrates rather to meet them in the field of politics than to maintain an attitude of philosophic superiority, and decline to encounter adversaries who were not worthy of his steel.

In a large society abstention from politics is a matter of choice. No one is seriously blamed for being what Americans call a "Mugwump." But the population of Athens formed a very small society; and Solon had made it actually punishable by law for a citizen to shirk the duties which fell on all alike in the absence of any system of representation ; even a silent aloofness was dangerous, and Socrates' abstention was not silent. Moreover, there must have been many who, like Callicles in the *Gorgias*, held philosophy to be but an idle pastime, permissible perhaps to youth, but not entitled to interfere with the serious political duties of later life ; least of all when, as in Socrates' case, the philosopher when he did appear stood forward as one

> qui libera posset
> verba animi proferre et vitam impendere vero.

Such was Socrates' attitude towards the politics of the day. But he touched public life in so far as he was the friend of certain prominent public men ; more especially in virtue of his intimacy with the brilliant Alcibiades. Some knowledge of the career of this remarkable man is almost a necessity for any one who wishes to appreciate Socrates' position by understanding the nature of those with whom he had to deal. Firstly, Alcibiades' history is closely bound up with the fortunes of that Athens in which Socrates lived and moved and had his being—while his character presents a type of those tendencies which directed Socrates' teaching and eventually determined his fate. Secondly, Alcibiades is more especially a representative of that young Athens to which the philosopher's instruction was throughout addressed, and with which to the end of his days he was closely associated.

To us, Alcibiades stands as the very impersonation of the brilliance and beauty, the extravagance, the rapid and transient success of the Athens of his day. Like his countrymen, he was endowed with extraordinary natural gifts; like them, he was the favourite of fortune; like them, he lost all through a combination of want of σωφροσύνη—moral balance and steadiness—and that jealousy which is naturally aroused by extraordinary success. From his earliest years his prospects were brilliant. His family was noble; his guardian—for his parents died while he was still a child—none other than the great Pericles. The stories told of him as a boy and a youth show him as the glass of fashion and the mould of form for young Athens—attractive in person and mind, and surrounded by a host of friends, flatterers, and parasites. When, shortly after the beginning of the Peloponnesian War, he made his *début* in the political arena, the same success attended him. He won distinction alike as a general and a diplomatist—in the latter capacity, it must be confessed, by ruses which most modern ministers would reject; but honesty was never a conspicuous virtue of Greek statesmen. He was the idol of the Athenian populace for his lavish munificence, and even for the very ostentation of his private luxury; even the severest censors were inclined to condone his personal laxities in consideration of his public liberality and the glory which his Olympian victories reflected on his native city. Moreover, that versatility which could assume every character at will must have enabled him to conciliate even men of widely-differing temperament. Catiline himself was not a greater adept at making himself all things to all men; he was more changeable (says Plutarch) than the chameleon.

About fifteen years after the commencement of the Peloponnesian War, Alcibiades' fame stood at its zenith; then, just when he seemed to be adding

the coping-stone to his greatness, the fabric col-
lapsed. It was the eve of the despatch of the
expedition to Sicily—a project which had been
undertaken by Athens principally at Alcibiades'
instigation, and in opposition to the soberer
counsels of older men like the veteran general
Nicias—and Alcibiades himself had been chosen
as one of the generals of the armament, and was
on the verge of departure; with what dreams of
an Empire of the West, which might have pro-
foundly modified the destinies of Carthage, nay
of Rome, perhaps, and the world, we can only
guess. At this moment untoward events were
reported in Athens. Sacrilege was rife; holy
mysteries had been burlesqued, sacred images
mutilated; and the voice of his enemies attributed
these crimes to Alcibiades and his friends. What
the facts were it is not likely that we shall ever
know. It appears to be true that Alcibiades
wished to have the matter sifted on the spot, so
that he might start on the expedition cleared and
unsuspected; but it is equally true that, when
the investigation, delayed by the action of his
political enemies, resulted in the despatch of a
summons to Alcibiades to return home and take
his trial, he feared to face his countrymen. This

episode marks the darkest chapter in a chequered biography. It was natural enough that Alcibiades should seek refuge as he did in flight; but his desertion to and service of Athens' bitterest enemies, the Spartans, is only an extreme mark of that want of principle which characterises all his career.

The later history of this remarkable genius is a record of continual intrigue. Leaving Laconia, where his brilliant abilities had enabled the Spartans not only to bring about the great Athenian disaster in Sicily, but to inflict further humiliation on Attica itself, he intrigued with Tissaphernes, the Persian governor of Western Asia Minor, over whom he exercised the same ascendency as over his own countrymen and the Spartans. Changing sides once more, he negotiated with the contending parties at Athens during a period of faction in such a way as to procure his return home, where the people seem to have received him as the saviour of his country; and it is certain that under his leadership Athens, deeply humiliated as she had been, began to regain something of her former position; throughout Alcibiades' career victory rested with that cause which he had temporarily made his own. But

D

after a time his own misconduct or the jealousy
of rivals destroyed his popularity, and he was once
more exiled, in an evil hour for his country; for
just as his defection had been followed by the
Sicilian disaster, so now the crushing capture of
the Athenian fleet at Aegospotami, which definitely
ended the long struggle of the Peloponnesian War,
was the sequel if not the result of his second
banishment. Nor did he long survive the fall
of his native city. He was obnoxious to Sparta;
it was the policy of Persia to humour the natural
leaders of Hellas; and eventually Alcibiades, who
had at different times been popular with all
parties—who had been the idol successively of
Athenians, Laconians, and Persians—ended his
life as the enemy of all three powers: exiled by
Athens, proscribed by Sparta, and murdered by
the hired swords of the Great King.

Once Alcibiades was embarked on the sea of
public life, we hear little of any intercourse with
Socrates; but in early youth he was one of the
great teacher's most constant pupils. Most of
Socrates' teaching is naturally addressed to young
men; he lived and moved among the young;
and no pupil could be more interesting than an
Alcibiades, with his supreme capacity for good

and evil—constantly surrounded by a court of admirers and flatterers, so that to obtain an ascendency over his character was a particularly piquant and notable triumph. According to Plutarch, Alcibiades oscillated between obedience to Socrates and to the persuasions of flattery The note of his youthful character was impressibility; "he was easily led to pleasure," says his biographer; yet at the same time he could be moved to tears by his mentor's discourses. Thus it was that, as Plutarch says, "just as iron is softened in the fire and then compressed and compacted in its several parts by cold, so whenever Socrates found Alcibiades frivolous and effeminate, he would subject him to the compression and contraction of reason, and thus made him humble and submissive by showing him his deficiencies and the imperfections of his virtue." This too is what one would gather from the two dialogues of Plato entitled *Alcibiades*. The *dramatis personae* are Socrates and Alcibiades— the argument, that of a philosopher grappling with the "deceitfulness of riches," and the many besetting dangers of Greek contemporary life. As we should say now, it is a match between the "Higher Life" and the world, the flesh, and the devil.

CHAPTER III

SOCRATES IN PLATO'S DIALOGUES: THE SOPHISTS

FOR the impression produced by Socrates on his contemporaries as a great and remarkable personage, there are three authorities, one of supreme, and two of secondary importance—Plato, Aristophanes, and Xenophon. It is more especially in Plato's dialogues that the only Socrates with whom we have any concern is revealed—that is, Socrates the conversationalist, the talker *par excellence* among a people of talkers. If he plays but a small part in history—so far as history is the chronicle of wars and political changes—he must evidently have been intimately connected with the social and intellectual development of Athens. That city was then, as she was five centuries later, always eager to hear or tell of some new thing. It was a period of intellectual awakening, when, as in the Elizabethan and in our own era, new ideas and new discoveries (dis-

coveries then, at least, of untrodden continents of
the intellect) were daily widening the field of
discussion. The vehicle of criticism was not writing
but conversation ; wit encountered wit in actual
speech. And several causes operated to make
Athens beyond all Greek towns a conversational
centre. Her political importance as well as her
theatrical exhibitions brought crowds of strangers
from all parts of Greece, the Aegean, nay from
the western outposts of Hellenic civilisation—from
Sicily itself and the Greek towns of Southern
Italy. Even the hardships of the Peloponnesian
War had their effect in this direction, as the fear
of the Peloponnesian raiders more and more
centralised Attic life within the walls of the
metropolis of Attica. So in Athens the most
diverse elements might find a meeting-place:
country gentlemen driven from their estates by
the terror of invading armies ; islanders bringing
tribute from the Aegean ; travelling professors
from Southern Italy or Asia Minor—all alike
contributing after their several fashions new points
of view and new elements of discussion.

It is this conversational habit of Athens which
lies at the root of Plato's dialogues. The form they
have taken is that of the talk of groups such as

daily gathered in the λέσχαι,—they are genuine
talk, not merely essays in dialogue form ; generally,
Plato has taken great pains to create the impression of real dialogues, in which the speakers are
usually not imaginary figures, but persons actually
known in the Athens of his day—an Alcibiades,
a Gorgias, an Aristophanes.   The *dramatis personae* are heterogeneous enough ; it was not Plato's
object to model his conversations after the closeted
discussions of any particular sect or clique, but
rather, as I have said, after such debates as might
arise in public places where men of all conditions
and beliefs would mostly congregate.   "Plato,"
says M. Taine in his essay on *Les Jeunes Gens de
Platon*, "put his syllogisms in conversations, and
made his theories a picture of manners.   Of all
philosophers, he alone has had the skill to give
life to his dissertations.   Malebranche's Theotimus
and Leibnitz' Philalethes are merely abstractions
with men's names.   They are fictions which take
away naturalness without adding an interest ; we
should much prefer the arguments by themselves,
without the *dramatis personae*.   The dialogue is
nothing but a borrowed ornament, an after-thought
added by an effort of imagination, to hide the
dryness of the subject and not alarm the reader.

But Plato's representations of character are drawn from life, and he has actually heard the conversations which he writes." Probably Taine would have included Xenophon under the same condemnation as Malebranche and Leibnitz. Xenophon's Socrates is too often a kind of personified *Mangnall's Questions:* the real man is too often invisible. A Xenophontic dialogue is not really like truth; the writer lacks the gift attributed by Aristotle to Homer of "lying as is necessary" (ψεύδεσθαι ὡς δεῖ). The true spirit of conversation is absent; the picture lacks vividness; it is to Plato that we look for such marvellously realistic descriptions as— thanks to the genius of the artist and the genius of the Greek language—we have in the opening and close of the *Symposium,* the introductory part of the *Protagoras,* and the final chapters of the *Phaedo.*

In all the dialogues Socrates is the most important speaker. This is not because Plato's chief purpose was always to record the sayings of Socrates; only the object of both men alike was discussion,—in Socrates' case oral, in Plato's written, —and so Socrates was an appropriate mouthpiece for the expression of Platonic opinion. Plato himself was one of the philosopher's youngest

hearers. He had no doubt often assisted at Socratic
séances in the latter half of the Peloponnesian War,
while the Laconian armies were harrying Attica,
or the Athenians were fighting, first for empire and
then for life, under the walls of Syracuse. One may
suppose—if it be not presumptuous to speculate
on the genesis of the dialogues—that Plato was
first moved to write by the desire of recording
things actually heard, or discussing some subject
in the way suggested by a discourse at which he
had been present ; and that as time went on he
departed more and more from personal reminiscence,
and used the name of Socrates in dramatising his
own speculations. But it is hard, if not impossible,
to draw a line and say that this doctrine is of
Socrates, that of Plato. Nor indeed are we much
concerned with that. Our business is rather, so
far as possible, to gather from Plato some picture
of the man Socrates—to learn how he spoke and
acted among the Athenians of his day. To this
end, Plato is our best guide ; as in the evolution
of his dialogues there emerge of necessity continual glimpses of a personality too striking and
too consistent to be other than real.

The Platonic Socrates is represented as an
elderly man (but in some dialogues he is evidently

still in the prime of manhood); loved and revered
by his immediate circle of friends; poor and
unpretentious in his habit of life, yet the equal
and friend of many celebrities; in argument,
of an irresistible force, and excelling most in
dialectic (that is, argument by the question of
method and answer); in physiognomy, the very
reverse of the conventional Greek type of beauty.
Further, Socrates no doubt belongs to a class of
men which plays a large part in the intellectual
history of the time—I mean the class of teachers
or "sophists."

The period of Socrates' life was perhaps the
most remarkable that the world has yet seen.
Through the seventy years from 469 to 399 B.C.
Athens was creating a new art and a new literature; creating, not merely developing from an
already subsisting inheritance; for the sculpture
of the age before Phidias and the pre-Aeschylean
drama—so far as tradition allows us to speak of
the latter at all—were far less nearly akin to the
masterpieces of the fifth century than Livius
Andronicus to Virgil, or Piers Plowman to Shakspeare. And the subsequent progress was as
rapid as the creation was startlingly sudden—
Euripides was only a younger contemporary of

Aeschylus, yet so diverse in style and though
that at times we seem to hear a poet of our own
century; Thucydides, only a few years subsequen
to Herodotus, yet in mental attitude so far removed
from him that at what we generally regard as the
world's usual rate of progress, five hundred year.
would be a not unnatural interval between the
older and the younger historian.

To an age which had accomplished a succession
of triumphs so rapid and in such diverse kinds, i
is not surprising that nothing should have seemed
too hard for the human intellect to attain. Amid
such invention and progress—"that which man
had done but earnest of the things which he should
do"—it was natural that men should believe that
success in any department was simply a matter of
teaching. In a certain sense it was the golden
age of education ; Greece was inundated by itinerant instructors in every art, —were it the art of war
or the art of rhetoric, or the art of virtue,—men
whose business was to "make wise," in short to
teach : the word "sophist," on which Plato's contempt for the less worthy among the pretenders
to the title has grafted so invidious a connotation
does really mean nothing worse than a teacher.
To us—even now, when it has been shown over

and over again that σοφιστής itself implies no
possible censure—it is impossible to use the term
without a suggestion at least of disrespect ; probably as long as the English language lasts " sophist "
will mean for us something very different from
what its Greek equivalent did to a Greek. Yet
nothing can be more unjust than to be misled by
the ideas which have gathered round this word ;
to imagine that σοφιστής was a term of reproach ;
or to place really great teachers—as, for instance,
Gorgias and Prodicus were in the estimation of
their contemporaries—in the same category as
mere quibblers such as Plato presents in his pictures of a Dionysodorus and an Euthydemus.
However, a class is far too often judged by
the conduct of its least respectable members ; and
as in the present instance Plato has not spared
some of even the greatest names, one can hardly
be surprised that the sophistical teaching should
be identified by posterity with the construction of
useless or even harmful fallacies.

Socrates was a teacher ; but not, like others,
by profession. He practised as an amateur, not
taking money for his teaching, and not travelling like most others and lecturing formally to
assembled audiences, but using such occasions as

were given him by casual encounters in the streets of Athens or conversation at some dinner-table. Nothing could be more informal than his method. The very name by which it is known, " Dialectic," implies not a monologue but a conversation, the argument being conducted by means of question and answer : it is more effective than monologue, in that it not only postulates but proclaims the interlocutor's assent every step in the process.

But the difference between Socrates and most other sophists went far deeper than this. As every period of construction involves also a proportionate amount of destruction, it was impossible that the new literature of the fifth century should be created without causing even the less reflecting Athenian public to be sensible of the shock to their traditional religion and morality. Old superstitions were vanishing and old legends discredited ; a spirit of universal questioning—the " What say you ? " which, as Aristophanes says, was continually on the lips of young Athens—was in the air ; antiquity was no longer safe in its stronghold of traditional reverence, but must stand on its defence against the philosophic doubt of a younger generation. But doubt must give place to belief of some kind ; and the thousand teachers of Hellas—

able or incompetent, sincere or insincere—were present to offer an immediate substitute for the worn-out ideas and methods of past centuries. As far as we can gather from Xenophon and Plato, Socrates' position with regard to this conflict of new and old was that of a conservative in the truest sense. It did not follow that because much of the old was admittedly bad, all of the new was necessarily good ; both alike were open to question ; the function of the true philosopher was to "prove all things, hold fast that which is good "—to attain truth by an earnest and careful consideration of the real nature of words and things. If everything was on its trial, the new teaching could claim no exception to the general rule ; to follow accepted tradition blindly was not more irrational than to be dazzled by the novelty of a reconstruction of society in a course of six lectures. To be misled by nothing, neither by prejudice nor "winds of doctrine," but to pursue unhampered and unchecked the investigation of things as they really are—that was the task which Socrates set himself. Xenophon says of him that he was continually inquiring into the real meaning of common terms.

It could not be expected that independent research should not bring the researcher into occasional collision with hasty reformers as well as with obscurantists: as the mass of conservatism at Athens was not in sympathy with Socrates, so he is continually quarrelling with his contemporaries' crude liberalism. But it would of course be absurd to suppose that he himself entertained that contempt for other sophists which later ages too hastily adopted from some parts of the Platonic dialogues: in fact Socrates once at least styles himself a sophist, without irony or suspicion of dispraise.

CHAPTER IV

THE BETTER TEACHERS OF THE TIME: GORGIAS AND PROTAGORAS

As Xenophon says, it was Socrates' principal desire to investigate the real meaning of words and the real nature of things; for which purpose he would naturally appeal if possible to the chief exponent of whatever subject was for the moment under inquiry. So, in the dialogue called *Gorgias*, the original theme of discussion is Rhetoric, and the individual to whom Socrates' first inquiries are addressed is the foremost living teacher of Rhetoric—Gorgias, a distinguished Sicilian professor of eloquence, himself not only a theorist but a practical speaker, whose name is mentioned in connection with contemporary politics. This person belongs to the maligned class of "sophists," but Plato describes him without any apparent animus against himself individually. His only fault appears to be that he has, naturally enough, too thorough a belief in his own trade,—there is nothing, he thinks, like rhetoric,—and that he is unprepared and therefore unable to cope with Socrates' dialectic when the latter goes back to first principles and questions the utility of professional eloquence. One may imagine that Gorgias considered the whole discussion rather futile, and thought Socrates merely a somewhat tiresome, unpractical person, inconveniently skilful in argument of a certain kind. He himself is a respectable figure enough ; only, according to Plato, he appears to less advantage in dialectic than in monologue, and is unable to resist the conclusions forced upon him by Socrates. Gorgias asserts the obvious truth that rhetoric is a good thing, but may be used for bad ends. Socrates proves—or argues in such a way that Gorgias cannot refute it—that the perfect rhetorician can have nothing to do with injustice.

" *G.* Whenever in respect of what you have mentioned, Socrates, there is a choice of alternatives, you see that it is the professional speaker who gives advice and whose advice is taken.

" *S.* Exactly ; that is what surprises me, and why I have long been trying to ascertain what is the power of rhetoric. Considered from our point of view, to me it seems as if it must be extraordinarily great.

"*G.* Yes, Socrates, and you would think so much more if you knew all—how it does, if I may say so, include in itself every kind of power. I will give you a strong proof of this. I have often gone with my brother or some other physician to see some sick man who would not take medicine or allow himself to be operated upon by incision or cautery; and where the physician failed to persuade I have succeeded, simply by the art of rhetoric and no other. Nay more—take any city you wish; if a professional speaker and a physician came to it and had to appear before the Ecclesia or any other body and state their respective claims for election to a medical post, the physician would be nowhere, and the capable speaker would be elected if he wished; and he would be better able than any one else to persuade the electors to choose himself, against whatever craftsman he were competing; for there is no subject about which the rhetorician cannot speak to a large audience more convincingly than any other professional man. Such and so great is the power of my art. Yet of course, Socrates, rhetoric should be used like any other method of fighting.

E

A trained combatant must not use his skill against
every one simply because he has learnt how to
box or to wrestle or to use weapons so well as to
be superior to friends or foes : that is no reason
why he should strike his friends or stab them to
death. But mark—if a man acquires good condition and skill in boxing by frequenting a training school and then beats his father and his
mother or any other relation or friend, that is no
reason why the trainers and teachers of the art of
fence should be detested and expelled from our
cities. For although the strength and skill is
abused and misapplied, it was imparted that it
might be employed for just ends, not for offence
but for defence, against enemies and aggressors.
It does not follow that the teacher and his art
are bad and blameworthy ; no, the fault is with
those who misuse his teaching. The same holds
good of rhetoric. The professional speaker can
make a better speech than any one else on any
topic—that is, he can better convince a large
audience on practically any subject he pleases ;
but the fact of his being able to discredit phy-
sicians or other professional men is no reason
why he ought to do so : he should use his art
of rhetoric for just ends, as the fighter should use

his art of fence. And surely if a man learns
rhetoric and then employs this power and art
unjustly, it is not the teacher whom we ought to
detest and expel from our cities ; for the instruction was meant to be used justly, though the
learner has misapplied it. It is not the teacher,
but the person who uses the teaching wrongly,
who deserves banishment or death."

At this point the discourse is broken for a
moment by one of those interruptions which prevent it from degenerating into a sham dialogue,
a disquisition in question and answer form, and
vividly recall Plato's intention of depicting a real
colloquy of real persons. "I am bound to say,"
Socrates puts in, "that I am not quite satisfied
with your arguments. Before, however, I try to
refute them I should like to know whether you,
Gorgias, are a disputant of my sort. Now I am
always for a serious argument without fear or
favour. Shall we thresh the matter out thoroughly
or not?" "Certainly," replies Gorgias, "provided
the gentlemen present have time to listen." Here
one may suppose there are cries of "Go on," and
Chaerephon explains that no one present has
any other wish but to hear an argument between
two such champions. Thus encouraged, Socrates

proceeds : "I will tell you, Gorgias, what it is that surprises me in what you have said ; for I dare say your meaning is right, and the fault mine in failing to understand you. You tell me, do you not, that you can give to any one who will learn of you a knowledge of the art of speaking? *G.* Yes. *S.* Then you can make him speak convincingly to a crowd by persuasion, not by instruction? *G.* Certainly. *S.* Now you said that a professional speaker will speak more convincingly than a physician on the question of health. *G.* Yes, I said so; that is, if he has a crowd for audience. *S.* By a crowd you mean, I suppose, a number of ignorant persons ; he will not, I presume, convince experts more than a physician would. *G.* That is true. *S.* Well, if he is more convincing than a physician, does not that mean that he is more convincing than an expert? *G.* Certainly. *S.* And he is not a physician, is he? *G.* That is so. *S.* Now I presume the person who is not a physician is ignorant on those matters of which a physician has knowledge. *G.* Clearly. *S.* Then, whenever the professional speaker is more con-vincing than the physician, that means that the ignorant man speaking to an ignorant audience is more convincing than a man of knowledge. Can we draw any other conclusion? *G.* That is the conclusion, in the present instance. *S.* Well, then, in all other arts the relation of the speaker and his art is the same; rhetoric need never know facts, only it must have invented a sort of engine of persuasion, which makes it appear to the ignorant to know more than an expert.

" *G.* Well, Socrates, is it not a very lucky thing for a man to be as good as experts in all other branches without having learnt anything but the one art of rhetoric? *S.* Whether this puts the rhetorician on an equality with other men or not is a point which we will presently consider, if it help our discussion; for the present this must be the subject of examination :—Is the professional speaker in the same case with regard to justice, beauty, goodness, and their contraries, as he is with regard to the subject-matter of the arts, such as health? that is, being ignorant of the facts and not knowing what is good or bad, beautiful or ugly, just or unjust, has he invented a way of persuading about these subjects so as to seem to an audience of ignorant persons to know more than an expert? Or must he be an expert in these matters, and must intending pupils in rhetoric be already provided with this knowledge when they come to you,—failing which, *you* cannot indeed instruct aspirants in subjects like these without travelling outside the province which is yours as a teacher of rhetoric, but will as a substitute give them a semblance of knowledge and a semblance of goodness quite sufficient to impose on the many? Or shall we say that you cannot teach rhetoric at all unless your pupil starts with a true knowledge of justice and the like? Tell us, Gorgias, what we are to believe,—do tell us without disguise, as you promised just now, what is the real function of rhetoric. *G.* Well, Socrates, my own opinion is that if the pupil knows nothing of these matters he will learn them from me as well as rhetoric.

"*S.* Good; now remember that. If you are to teach a man rhetoric, he must either know before what is just and unjust, or learn from you afterwards. *G.* Certainly. *S.* Well! is not a man who has learnt carpentry a carpenter? *G.* Yes. *S.* And a man who has learnt music is a musician? *G.* Yes. *S.* And a man who has learnt medicine a physician? And in fact it holds good throughout, does it not, that whatever you learn you resemble the object of your science? *G.* Certainly it does. *S.* By this rule, then, a man who has learnt justice is just. *G.* Assuredly. *S.* Now the just man, I suppose, acts justly. *G.* Yes. *S.* Then it follows that the student of rhetoric must be just—and the just man wishes to act justly. *G.* It would appear so. *S.* Then the just man will never wish to act with injustice. *G.* Indisputably. *S.* Remember that our argument showed that the rhetorician must be just. *G.* Yes. *S.* Then the rhetorician will never wish to act with injustice. *G.* So it would appear.

" *S.* Well, do you remember saying just now that we ought not to blame or banish trainers if a boxer uses the art of boxing for unjust purposes ? And in the same way that if a professional speaker uses the art of rhetoric unjustly, it is not the teacher who should be censured and banished, but the pupil who acts unjustly and so misuses his art ? Did you not say that ? *G.* I did. *S.* Yet now it is proved that the same person, I mean the professional speaker, can never act unjustly. *G.* That is so."

So far, Socrates is only a clever dialectician. His real intention is not revealed until Gorgias has retired from the conversation, which is taken up by his pupil Polus, himself a teacher of rhetoric, young in years and impetuous in argument. The subject is now the value of oratory. Orators,

Polus asserts, are powerful ; and power is happiness. No, answers Socrates ; not if it be power combined with injustice. To be unjust and unpunished is the lowest depth of misery. If rhetoric protects the unjust from punishment, it is but increasing the sum of unhappiness.

"In my judgment, Polus," says Socrates, "the doer of wrong and injustice must in any case be unhappy ; yet he is so to a greater degree if he pays no penalty and escapes punishment for his wrongdoing, and to a less degree if he is punished by gods and men."

Polus makes the natural reply that this is a strange paradox. "Why, how mean you? Suppose a man be taken in the act of wrongful usurpation of despotism, and, being taken, be racked, mutilated, and blinded, and after not only suffering all kinds of terrible outrages to his own person, but witnessing their infliction on members of his own family, be at last crucified or burnt in pitch : is such a fate more fortunate than to succeed in usurpation, and live and rule as an autocrat, envied and deemed happy by citizens and aliens? Is this your paradox which you defy me to disprove?" Socrates replies : "My excellent Polus, you are trying to frighten me with a bogey, instead of

disproving my statement as you assured me you
would. Still, just as a reminder, tell me if you
did not use the expression 'unjust usurpation of
despotism'? *P.* I did. *S.* Well, I answer that
neither of your supposed persons can be called
more fortunate, neither he who succeeds in his
unjust usurpation, nor he who is punished for the
attempt : they are both miserable, and so neither
can be more fortunate than the other ; but of the
two the successful usurper is the more miserable.
What, Polus! you laugh ? Is that another of your
refutations, to turn what is said into ridicule
without disproving it? *P.* Why, Socrates, do you
not see that you are refuted out of your own
mouth, when you uphold what is contrary to
every one's opinion ? Ask any one here present.
S. I am none of your politicians, Polus. Last
year I was chosen a member of the Senate, and
when my tribe had the presidency, and it was my
duty to take the votes, I was laughed at for not
knowing how to do it. So do not ask me to take
the votes here either : if you have no better
disproof than that, let me take my turn, and you
shall see what I consider to be a proper form of
disproof. I know how to produce one witness to
the truth of my assertion—I mean my interlocutor

—but I care nothing for the general public. I know how to take one man's vote; but with your 'general public' I would not even hold converse."

Polus is thus led on, through a maze of skilfully-put questions to which he cannot refuse assent, to admit at last the truth of his antagonist's paradox, "That the wrongdoer is always miserable, and most miserable of all when he goes unpunished."

"Well then," Socrates concludes, "if all this is true, where, Polus, is the great need for rhetoric? From our present conclusions it follows that what it is our duty to guard against is the committing of injustice on our own part, for we know that the act will bring its own sufficient punishment. Is not that so? *P.* Certainly. *S.* Yes; and if you yourself or any one near and dear to you commit a wrong, you must voluntarily resort to the quarter where punishment will be most speedily inflicted: you must consult the judge, I mean, as you would a physician, and take special care that the disease of wrong does not become inveterate, and so develop an incurable canker within the soul. What are we to say, Polus, if our recent conclusions hold good? Is it not only on this assumption that the earlier and later parts of our argument will harmonise? *P.* It must be admitted, Socrates.

S. Rhetoric, then, is noway serviceable for defend-
ing the commission of wrong whether by yourself,
or your parents, or friends, or children, or country.
Quite the contrary: its only use is in accusation,
on the hypothesis that it is your duty to accuse
any wrongdoer among your family and friends,
and still more so if the wrongdoer be yourself;
that you should attempt no concealment, but bring
the wrong to light, that the perpetrator may be
punished and so cured ; that you should compel
the wrongdoer, be he yourself or another, not to
shrink like a craven, but submit in manly silence,
as to the operating knife or cautery of a
physician, pursuing after the good and beautiful
without regard of pain, and voluntarily submitting
to whatever penalty the wrong deserves, be it
scourging, imprisonment, fine, exile, or death, and
being thus the leading counsel for the prosecution
of yourself and your friends, and so using the art
of rhetoric—I mean, that you or they may have
the wrong fully exposed, and thus be rid of
injustice, which is the worst of all evils."

Socrates' position now becomes what it remains
through the rest of the dialogue—that of the philosopher who contemns and defies the judgments of
the world around him. This attitude is further

illustrated by his argument with a third opponent, Callicles. This person asserts cynically that it is not rhetoric but philosophy that is useless; that pleasure is the only good, might right, man's true ideal the gratification of all his desires.

"When I see a boy who is still of an age to talk in this way, lisping childish jokes, I am pleased,— I think it elegant and gentlemanly, and befitting the lad's tender years; but if I hear him regularly arguing, it is unpleasant and painful to listen to; it is in some sort degrading to a free man: and so when we hear and see a man lisping and playing with words, we think he is doing a ridiculous and childish thing, and needs correction. Now just this is what I, for my part, think of students of philosophy. It is a laudable and proper study in a young boy, for then alone is he really free; without such study he will be illiberal, and can never aspire to anything fair or noble; but an older man who will still be philosophising seems to me, Socrates, to deserve corporal punishment. For, as I said just now, such a man, be he ever such a genius, must of necessity lose his manliness—he will shun the centres and public places of the city, where, as the poet says, men win fair renown; he sneaks away and lives all his life whispering to three or four lads in a corner; he never utters any liberal, great, satisfactory sentiment.

"Now, Socrates, I am your friend, as I ought to be. You and I are, I conceive, like Amphion and Zethus (whom I mentioned just now) in Euripides' play. For I am moved to use the same language to you as Zethus does to his brother, and to say: You neglect, Socrates, what should be your chiefest care; you trick the noble nature of your soul with boylike semblance; you cannot play a wise adviser's part in counselling of justice, nor can list to rede of right and reason, nor can plan with vigour to assist your fellow-man. Now, my dear Socrates, you will not be angry with me, as I speak out of goodwill to you. But are you not ashamed of that condition which I conceive to be yours, and that of those who will still be going deeper into philosophy? For as you now are, if you, or any one like you, were arrested and haled off to prison on a false charge of wrongdoing, you know that you would be quite helpless; you would be dizzy and dumfounded for lack of words; and when brought into court, however mean and worthless your accuser, you would be condemned to death if that were the penalty he demanded.

"Now, Socrates, how can the name of wisdom be

given to an art which depraves the gifts that are
innate in men, so that they cannot help themselves,
cannot save themselves or any one else from the
greatest perils ; but can be robbed of all their property by their enemies, and be members of the
State without possessing any of its rights ? for that
is what they are. Such a one as these—if you will
forgive the bluntness of my expression—any one
may smite on the check without fear of punishment. Nay, sir, be ruled by me ; cease from your
quibbles ; study skill in action ; study to win
a name for sound sense ; leave to others these
subtleties (chatter or folly, call it which you will),
which will but make your dwelling desolate ; and
emulate, instead of your choppers of paltry logic,
men who have substance and reputation and many
other good things."

By refuting Callicles' assertion, Socrates em-
phasises his former paradox — that unpunished
injustice is the worst of all evils to the unjust.
It is a contrast of ideals ; the object of Callicles
and his like is pleasure : the object of the philosopher is order and control in the State and the
individual. To him, the unpunished criminal is
far more miserable than the good man suffering
wrongfully. Therefore, there is no point in

Callicles' scoffs at the unpractical character of philosophy. And, if results are to be taken into account, what—Socrates asks—has been the fate of your "practical politicians," your Athenian statesmen? They met with various disasters at the hands of their citizens; which shows that they were incompetent as educators of their countrymen— that is, as politicians. In fact, the only true politician is the philosopher, who has nothing to do with "politics" at all. He may, perhaps, suffer for his antagonism to the worser kind of public opinion. But there are other tribunals besides those of this world; and Socrates thus puts the finishing touch to his answer of Callicles —*more suo*—by the apologue which describes the Last Judgment.

"I would have you lythe and listen,' as the saying goes, to an account which you, I suppose, will call fabulous, but which I hold historical; for I am assured of the truth of what I am going to tell you. According to Homer, Zeus and Poseidon and Pluto made a division of their sovereignty as soon as they inherited it. Now in Cronos' time there was a law in heaven respecting mankind, which law indeed exists now as it has from eternity, to the effect that those who have lived a just and virtuous life shall after death depart to the isles of the blest, and there dwell untroubled in perfect happiness; while those who have passed unjust and godless lives shall go to that place of doom and punishment which is the prison called Tartarus. Under Cronos, and in the early part of Zeus' reign, men were judged while still alive, on the day when they were to die, and by judges themselves living. So justice miscarried; wherefore Pluto, and the governors of the isles of the blest coming therefrom, told Zeus that men undeserving of their fate were continually sent to either place. 'Nay,' said Zeus, 'but I will make an end of this. For now the cases are ill-tried: they that are judged come clothed before the judgment-seat, being still in life. Many therefore who have evil souls are clothed with fair bodies, high lineage, or wealth, and on the day of their judgment they bring many witnesses to testify to the righteousness of their lives, whereby the judges are confounded; and moreover they are themselves clothed while they give judgment, for that their soul wears before it the veil of eyes and ears and all the bodily parts. Thus are they blinded by their own clothing and the clothing of those whom they judge. First, then, mankind must lose that

foreknowledge of death which they now have;
and I have instructed Prometheus how to make
this no longer a part of them. Next, they must
be judged after death, and so naked; and the
judge must himself be dead and naked likewise,
seeing with his very soul the very soul of those
whom he judges, immediately after their death,—
kinsfolk and the pomp and circumstance of life
all left behind on earth; for thus only can the
judgment be just. All this I saw before you; and
I have therefore made judges of three of my sons,
Minos and Rhadamanthus from Asia, and Aeacus
from Europe. These after death shall hold their
court in the mead, at the parting of the ways,
whence one road leads to the isles of the blest
and the other to Tartarus. There the dead of
Asia shall be judged by Rhadamanthus, and the
dead of Europe by Aeacus. Minos I will make
supreme arbiter, to decide when the other two
are at fault: that so most justly it may be determined by which way the souls of men shall
travel.'

"Such, Callicles, is what I have heard and believe to be true; and from this account I draw
the following conclusions :—Death is to my mind
simply the separation of the soul from the body.

F

Whenever the process of separation is over, each
of the two parts retains almost unaltered that
habit which belonged to it in life: the body still
manifesting its fashion and its marks of tending
and suffering. When the body has in life been
naturally tall or artificially developed, the corpse
is still tall in death; and so when it has been fat,
and so forth. Or again, where long hair was worn,
the corpse too is longhaired. Again, if a man has
in life been scourged, and borne such marks of
blows as scars of wounds, whether inflicted by the
lash or otherwise, these marks remain on his body
after death; and limbs broken or distorted during
life present the same appearance when life is over;
in short, the body retains for a time after the end
of its life all or most of those characteristics with
which it was invested while living. The same
applies to the soul: as soon as it is stripped of
the body all its characteristics come into view—
its natural constitution, and the affections which
result from particular pursuits. So, when the
dead come before the judge, who if they are of
Asia will be Rhadamanthus, he sets them there
and examines each soul without knowing whose
it is; and often he lays hands on the Great King
or some other monarch or potentate only to dis-

cover that the soul is nowhere free from blemish,
but striped and scarred by perjury and wrong, and
branded with all the marks of personal conduct;
all distorted by falsehood and vanity, and deformed
by the untruths of its upbringing; rendered ugly
and misshapen by habits of power, luxury, arro-
gance, and licence. Such a soul the judge regards
with contempt, and sends straightway to that prison
where it is to undergo the proper penalties. Now
it is proper that all right punishment should either
improve and benefit its victim, or make him such
a public example as may alarm others into a better
way of living by the spectacle of his sufferings.
When the offence committed is curable, punishment inflicted by gods or men is beneficial (yet
only beneficial by pain and anguish whether in
this world or the next; for thus alone can wrong
be done away). But the public examples are
those heinous offenders whose sins have rendered
them incurable; these being incurable cannot
themselves receive any benefit from their punishment; but they can be serviceable to others who
see the eternity of terrible torment which is the
consequence of sin; such sinners do indeed serve
as examples, fast bound in the prison-house of
Hades for a spectacle and a warning to all the

unjust who come thither. Such to my mind is
the fate of Archelaus (if we are to believe Polus),
and other despots like him. These examples are,
I think, oftenest seen in the persons of despots,
kings, potentates, and statesmen : it is they who
are guilty of the worst and most abominable
crimes, because of the power which they have.
This is borne out by Homer, in whose poems it
is the kings and potentates, a Tantalus or a
Sisyphus or a Tityus, who suffer eternal punishment. Sinners of lower estate, such as Thersites,
are nowhere represented as undergoing the grievous
penalties of incorrigible criminals : it was the
power, as we may suppose, that was wanting to
them, and in this respect they were more fortunate
than those who had it.

"No, Callicles ; great wickedness is the natural
outcome of great power; although the combination
of virtue with power is not impossible, and is most
admirable when it occurs ; for to be consistently
just when there are no obstacles to injustice is an
achievement of great difficulty, and deserves the
highest praise. Few indeed are capable of it.
Yet there have been and will be, both here and
elsewhere, instances of supreme excellence in that
righteous discharge of a trust, for which Aristides

son of Lysimachus won the pre-eminent admiration
not only of Athens but all Hellas. But the general
rule is, that power begets vice.

"To resume: when Rhadamanthus finds some
such souls as I have described, he knows neither
their names nor their lineage, but only the fact of
their wickedness. This he clearly perceives, and
therefore despatches them to the nether pit, with
a mark to show whether he deems them curable
or the reverse: thither they go, and suffer the
proper punishment. But sometimes he comes
upon a soul that has lived a life of justice or truth,
in high or low estate (and it is more likely, as I
think, that such will have belonged to a philosopher
who has lived to himself alone and not meddled
with the affairs of others); this soul Rhadamanthus
regards with admiration, and sends away to the
isles of the blest. Thus he does, and Aeacus does
likewise. Both of them hold a wand as they sit
in judgment; Minos, who presides, alone has a
golden sceptre : as Odysseus in Homer saw him—

Holding a sceptre of gold while the doom of the dead he
declareth.

"For my part, Callicles, I believe this account;
and my aim is to make my soul as free from
blemish as may be against the day when the judge

shall see it. I am minded, then, to care nothing for
what the world calls honour, but to regard truth
alone ; and so to live, and die when death comes,
with what real goodness I can. To live this life
and fight this battle (for there is none so well
worth the fighting), I earnestly exhort all others,
and offer you this counsel in return for yours to
me : and I say it is a shame for you that, when
you face the trial and judgment I have described,
you will be unable to help yourself ; so that when
you appear before the Aeginetan judge and he
lays hands on you to hale you away, you will be
then as speechless and bewildered as I am in your
courts here; and perchance you will be smitten
foully on the cheek and every way maltreated."

Callicles himself is not an interesting figure.
He is deeply imbued with what he considers to be
a practical man's contempt for speculation and its
outcome : himself thoroughly immoral, he does not
understand the beauty of goodness and the ugliness
of evil ; and a very little provocation drives him
to the crudest assertion of extremes. But he has
no power of argument. He is throughout angry
with Socrates, and eventually refuses even to
answer him, when he is evidently getting the worst

of it. Still, the Calliclean part of the dialogue is supremely interesting, because Socrates' attitude is a foreshadowing of his own end, when he "suffered for righteousness' sake," and did not therefore esteem himself unhappy. Throughout the *Gorgias* there breathes the spirit of tranquil and defiant martyrdom.

There is certainly no similarity between Socrates and St. Simeon Stylites. Yet perhaps there is no part of Greek classical literature which gives clearer expression than does the *Gorgias* to the great theory of purification by suffering in this world— that moving idea which kindled the fires of the Inquisition, as well as encouraging the constancy of its victims. It is easy to contrast pagan with Christian religious sentiment, if you take Theocritus to represent the one side and St. Francis of Assisi the other, and to show how far removed was classical Hellas from mediævalism. Yet, to which extremity is Socrates nearest? Certainly St. Francis' "Praised be my Lord for our sister the death of the body" would have been understood by no Greek of the Socratic period. But in that "otherworldliness" which absolutely rejects the human standard, and either "takes no account of pain" or even considers it a necessary purifica-

tion and preparation for future happiness, Socrates
is united in belief with the monk of the desert and
the martyr of the arena.

None of the itinerant professors of Hellas enjoyed a greater reputation in Socrates' day than
Protagoras of Abdera. For some forty years he
was held in high esteem as a "teacher of virtue";
and so it was natural that when Plato undertook
to make the Teachableness of Virtue the subject
of a dialogue, he should have "coupled the subject
with the name" of Protagoras.

Like other dialogues, the *Protagoras* is a drama,
not lacking in incident. Just as Lessing has shown
how in the Homeric poems (as indeed in all
really good art) there is no such thing as description for its own sake, independent of the course
of events, but the necessary details of the *mise en
scène* are developed and set forth by the narrative
as it proceeds : just so, in Plato, the conversation
is made to grow naturally out of circumstances.
We begin to read a story, and are insensibly introduced to a dialogue. The parties in this colloquy
are persons historically as well as artistically real,
some of them still familiar figures to the Hellas
of Plato's day ; and philosophic inquiry never

escapes from the local circumstances and individual peculiarities which colour it at the outset. As is often the case, Socrates himself is the narrator, reporting the story of his *rencontre* with Protagoras to an unnamed friend; how he heard by chance of the famous teacher's arrival at Athens, and how he found him among other intellectual giants discoursing to a crowd of listeners : the whole prologue at once presenting a charmingly picturesque scene of Greek life, and forming a most artistically designed prelude to the encounter of great wits which is to follow.

"This last night, while it was still very early in the dawning, I heard some one knocking violently at the door with a stick. It was Hippocrates, Apollodorus' son, Phason's brother. When the door was opened he hurried in, crying in a great voice, 'Are you awake, Socrates, or asleep?' I said, 'Why, here is Hippocrates; have you any news?' 'No, none,' he replied, 'but good news.' 'Tell them then,' I said. 'What is your news, and what brings you here at this hour?' He came and stood by me and said, 'Protagoras has arrived' (coming close and standing by me). 'That was the day before yesterday,' I replied; 'and have you only just heard?' 'Only yesterday evening,' he said. Groping for the bed, he sat down by my feet, and continued: 'Yes, in the evening, after coming back very late from Oenoe. Satyrus, my slave, had run away; I intended to tell you that I should pursue him, but something put it out of my head. On my return, after we had dined and were going to bed, my brother told me that Protagoras was here. Even then I was for going straight to you, but on second thoughts it seemed too late at night; so as soon as I had slept off my fatigue I got up at once and came hither as you see.' I recognised his manly ardour and excitement, and asked him, 'Why, what is this to you? Have you anything against Protagoras?' 'I have, indeed, Socrates,' he answered, with a smile; 'he is the only wise man, and will not make me wise too.' 'You are wrong,' I replied; 'certainly he will, if you pay him and persuade him.' 'I wish to heaven,' he said, 'it may only depend on that: I will spend all my own and my friends' money on him. But that is just why I have come to you now, to ask you to speak with him for me: I am too young, and besides, I have never seen Protagoras nor heard him. I was only a child when he was here the first time. You know, Socrates,

every one praises him and says he is the cleverest
speaker! let us go to him at once, so as to catch
him at home : he is lodging, as I heard, with
Callias, the son of Hipponicus. Come!' 'Not yet,
my friend,' I said, 'it is too early ; let us go out
here into the court, and walk about till it is light ;
then we can go to him. Protagoras is generally
indoors; don't be afraid, we shall probably find
him in.' "

So Socrates and the young Hippocrates turn
out into the court, and discourse on the danger of
putting yourself in the hands of a teacher until
you know what he is to teach you—the calm
prudence of Socrates in strong contrast to the
youthful enthusiasm of his companion—and presently they go to Protagoras' lodging.

"When we came to the porch, we stopped and
discussed some question which had arisen on the
way. So, as we did not wish to go in before
coming to some conclusion, we halted and continued our conversation until we had agreed. The
porter, I suppose, must have heard us, and I
dare say he thinks visitors troublesome, there are
so many sophists who come. At any rate, when
we knocked at the door, and he opened it and
saw us, he said, 'What, more sophists! he has no

time to see you,' and slammed the door to with
both hands as vehemently as he could. We
knocked again, and he answered us (from the
other side of the door), 'My good men, I have
told you already that he has no time.' 'Sir,' I
said, 'we are not come for Callias, and we are not
sophists; don't be afraid; it is Protagoras whom
we want to see. Please announce us.' So at last,
very reluctantly, he did open the door.

  *   *   *   *   *

 "When we were all seated, Protagoras said, ' Now
that our friends have come, Socrates, perhaps you
will speak further of the matter which you mentioned just now on behalf of this youth.' I replied,
'I can only begin, as I did then, by stating the
object of my coming. Hippocrates, who is here,
wishes to become your pupil,—and says that he
would like to hear what will be the result to himself of his learning from you. That is all that I
have to say.' 'Well, my young friend,' replied
Protagoras (speaking to Hippocrates), 'this is
what will happen to you if you become my pupil
—the first day you come to me you will return
home a better man, and so too on the next day:
you will improve steadily from one day to another.'
At this I said, 'What you tell him, Protagoras,

does not surprise me; it is perfectly natural; even you yourself, for all your age and wisdom, would improve if you were taught something which you do not know. Do not give us that answer. Suppose the case stood thus: suppose, for instance, that Hippocrates here were to change his mind and wish to become a pupil of this young Zeuxippus of Heraclea who is lately come among us, and were to go to him and be told by Zeuxippus what he is told by you, that every day he remained with him he would become better and improve; suppose he were then to ask: How do you say that I shall be better, and in what shall I improve? In painting, Zeuxippus would say. Or if he were to go to Orthagoras of Thebes and hear from him what he has heard from you, and were then to ask : In what respect shall I become daily better for learning from you? Orthagoras would reply: In flute-playing. So too this youth, and I his spokesman, have a plain question for you to answer. When Hippocrates here becomes Protagoras' pupil, he is to go away a better man for the first day's instruction, and so improve daily all the while; but how, Protagoras, and in what respect?'
'Your question, Socrates,' replied Protagoras, 'is a good one, and I am always glad to answer good

questions. If Hippocrates comes to me, he will find my treatment quite different from that of any other teacher. All others deal wrongly by their pupils: they put them perforce back to the school studies with which they have done already, and teach them mathematics and astronomy and geometry and music' (this with a glance at Hippias); 'but if he comes to me he will be taught nothing but what he has come to learn— lessons of prudence in domestic and public affairs —that is, on the one hand how best to govern his own house, and on the other how to be best able to serve the State by speech and action.' 'I conceive,' said I, 'unless I mistake your meaning, that you refer to the civic art, and undertake to make men good citizens.' 'That,' said he, 'is indeed exactly what I promise to do.'"

Socrates' own contention is—at least originally —that virtue is not teachable, a theory which deprives Protagoras of his *raison d'être;* and he invites the great man, who naturally supports the contrary opinion, to state his case. "Shall I do so," Protagoras asks, "by relating a story, or by argument?" "Whichever way you please," is the general answer. Protagoras then relates the myth which is intended to illustrate his doctrine by

accounting, as he says, for the fact that all men
have or should have some share of the "civic art,"
that art or virtue which enables communities of
men to exist.

" Once upon a time the gods existed, but mortal
beings not yet. And when the destined moment
arrived for their creation also, the gods moulded
them beneath the earth by mingling earth and
fire and such substances as result from the ad-
mixture of those elements. And when they were
ready to bring them up to the light, they charged
Prometheus and Epimetheus to equip the various
kinds and assign fitting faculties to each. But
Epimetheus asked leave from Prometheus to assign them himself, promising that Prometheus
should afterwards see and judge of his work.
Having gained his point he began the distribution,
and thus he made it :—to some kinds he gave the
property of strength without speed, while the
weaker creatures he provided with swiftness ; to
some he gave armour, while on others he bestowed
no natural weapon, but devised other means_ for
their protection. For those that he clad in little-
ness of stature he made to fly with wings or dwell
beneath the earth; and a like rule of compensation
held good throughout his assignment. All this

he devised because he was careful that no one
kind should be extirpated. And when he had
given them sufficient protection against mutual
destruction, he contrived a ready defence against
the seasons of heaven by clothing them with thick
hair and sturdy hides, sufficient to keep out cold
and heat,—intending too that these should stand
them in stead as their peculiar and native beddings
when they went to their lairs. Some he shod with
hoofs, some with hairy coverings and callous, blood-
less hides. Next he assigned to each kind its
peculiar nourishment : some he made to eat grass,
some the fruits of trees, some roots ; while some
again were to subsist by devouring other live
creatures. And to these last he gave only a
limited power of reproduction, while those that
were to be their prey he made prolific; thus he
provided against the extinction of the species.
Now Epimetheus was not excessively clever, and
so when the only kind yet unequipped was the
human race, he found that he had unawares used
up all the faculties, and he was at a loss what to
do. He being in this strait, Prometheus came to
judge of the assignment, and saw that while all
the other living creatures were suitably provided
with all things, man alone was naked and unshod,

unfurnished with bedding or weapons; although
the fated day had now arrived when he, like all
other creatures, must emerge from the earth into
light. Being therefore hard put to it for some
protection to devise for mankind, Prometheus stole
from Hephaestus and Athena their cunning in the
arts, and fire withal—for without fire none could
acquire or practise that craft—and then gave it to
men. So then they had cunning enough for self-
support but not for social intercourse; that art
was in the keeping of Zeus. Prometheus could
not go so far as into the citadel where Zeus dwelt,
fearing moreover the heavenly warders; but he did
go privily into the workshop wherein Hephaestus
and Athena together practised their arts, and stole
and delivered to man the secret of Hephaestus'
art of fire, and of Athena's skill in all other arts.
Thus was mankind provided with resource for its
livelihood; and by Epimetheus' fault Prometheus
afterwards suffered the recorded punishment of
his theft.

"Men, having thus been suffered to partake of
the divine nature, were the only living creatures
that believed in the gods, by reason of their kinship with them, and essayed to build them altars
and images; and they soon used their art to

G

invent articulate sounds and names, besides dwellings and raiment and shoes, bedding, and vegetable nutriment. Thus equipped, they dwelt at first in scattered habitations, and had no cities. Being then every way weaker than the beasts, they became their prey; man's skill in craftsmanship was sufficient to provide him with sustenance, but not to help him in his war with wild animals; for he had not yet that social or civic art of which the art of war is a branch. They were therefore fain to assemble together and found cities for their protection. So whenever they had thus assembled they would do each other wrong, inasmuch as they had not the civic art; wherefore they would disperse again and perish as before. Then, fearing lest mankind should be totally extirpated, Zeus sent Hermes with a gift to men of Honour and Justice, with the intent that these should set their cities in order and be bonds to unite them in amity. Hermes asked of Zeus in what manner Honour and Justice should be bestowed on mankind. 'Shall I,' he said, 'follow the fashion of the assignment of the arts? For in that assignment the rule has held that it is sufficient for one among many to be a physician or other craftsman. Shall I give men Honour and Justice by the like

rule, or shall I distribute the gift among all?'
'Among all,' replied Zeus; 'let all share the
gift, for were it divided among as few as those to
whom skill has been given in the arts, no cities
could be formed. Moreover, you shall give them
this law of my making: whosoever can have no
share of Honour and Justice is a disease in the
city, and must be therefore slain.'"

Protagoras himself is, like Gorgias, a teacher of
established and deserved reputation; nor does
Plato seriously wish to dethrone him. In fact
nothing to his discredit appears in the dialogue.
He is represented as a really brilliant speaker—
like the majority of his fellows, and like some
great talkers of modern times, something of a
lecturer—and a skilful arguer; much more so, and
a far more interested disputant, than the great
rhetorician. He is, in short, in some ways not
unlike Socrates himself—only, his inferior in hand-
ling the weapons of dialectic, and therefore pre-
ferring monologue. This dissimilarity between the
styles of the two principal speakers on one occasion
causes a difficulty, which nearly brings the conversation to a premature close, and has to be
smoothed away by the intervention of some of the

audience: Socrates objects to Protagoras' long speeches, which he says he cannot follow.

There is no dialogue in which the minor parts are played by more distinguished persons. Among them are Hippias and Prodicus—Hippias, the Leonardo da Vinci of the age, in Plato's view an altogether too versatile Admirable Crichton, who can make poetry as well as his own clothes—and Prodicus, the author of the really great fable called the *Choice of Heracles,* a teacher who enjoys the proud distinction of being known to the German criticism of fifty years ago as "the most innocent of the sophists." It is a conference of great educators, hard enough to parallel by anything in our modern life ; for assuredly it is neither a congress of University professors nor of head-masters. Perhaps a discussion among popular preachers would be nearer the mark. But the sophist was a phenomenon peculiar to the astonishing civilisation of Hellas : a reading public has annihilated him.

CHAPTER V

IT was the aim of Plato to confront opinion with opinion, to draw out and expose the fallacy of popular sophistical teachings and methods ; and for this no instrument could be more potent than the " Socratic irony "—that assumption of ignorance or philosophic doubt which invites instruction from any and every quarter ; Socrates meanwhile posing as the candid and guileless inquirer (the " Heathen Chinee " of speculation, if one may use a profane illustration); sometimes, as in the *Republic*, without any aim except to get at all sides of the question, but oftener with the intention of luring an adversary on into ostentatious displays of cleverness, that he may eventually be hopelessly entangled in the web of his own sophistries. And the irony is more complete when, as in the *Euthydemus*, the philosopher allows his interlocutors the maximum

85

of opportunity, and at the end leaves them
ostensibly masters of the field; exposed of course,
so far as readers are concerned, but for the moment
secure in the conceit of their own invincible skill.

The remarks of M. Taine above quoted are
true in general of the Platonic dialogues; but
they are not uniformly applicable. Sometimes,
after the almost invariable introductory details as
to the *mise en scène*, the *dramatis personae* are sub-
ordinated to the matter of the argument : were it
not for their occasional assent to questions less
real than "rhetorical," we might forget their
presence altogether, so little important are they to
the general theme. Such is the case, for instance,
in the *Laws* and in the greater part of the *Republic*. But the *Euthydemus* is a dialogue of an
entirely different kind. Socrates is no longer the
presiding genius of an assenting circle; he is a
hearer, a disputant; he will perhaps be a pupil,
should he be satisfied of the competence of his
masters. It is really a conversation, thoroughly
and *humanly* "eristic," in which the conversers
are real men; not assentient puppets, but wrang-
ling Greeks. Anger, pique, vanity, contempt, all
play their part in forming the course of the dispute. The whole scene is instinct with vitality:

one sees them—the conceited pair of "professors
of universal knowledge," proud of their verbal
technique, and with a professorial intolerance of
interruption ; the lad Clinias, modest, innocent,
obedient, but rather frightened and mystified by
the conjuring tricks of Euthydemus and Dionysodorus ; Ctesippus, the healthy young man who
looks at these things from a common-sense point
of view, and does not care to conceal his contempt
for people who prove to him that black is white ;
and Socrates himself, veiling to the end a ridicule
too deep for mere laughter under the mask of
an affected admiration for the sophists' skill. The
whole dialogue dramatises different points of view
as only Plato can do it.

The conversation is related by Socrates to his
friend and coeval Crito ; and grows out of a
chance meeting with Euthydemus and Dionysodorus, two itinerant teachers. This meeting is
described with every detail of scene and circumstance, as usual with Plato, who never allows us
to forget the "properties." " It so happened,"
says Socrates, "that I was sitting where you saw
me alone in the *apodyterium* [of the Lyceum,
a gymnasium in the eastern suburb of Athens
commonly resorted to by Socrates and his friends],

and I was just thinking of getting up; but as I did so I received the usual warning from my attendant genius (τὸ εἰωθὸς σημεῖον τὸ δαιμόνιον), so I sat down again. Presently came in those two, Euthydemus and Dionysodorus, and a great crowd with them, pupils as I suppose; and having come in they walked round in the covered promenade. ‚Before they had gone two or three times round, in comes Clinias (who you say rightly is much grown), followed by a number of his friends (ἐρασταί), among whom was Ctesippus, a youth of the Paianian deme, whose natural qualities leave nothing to be desired, except that he is so violent because he is young. So then Clinias saw me from the entrance, sitting alone, and he came straight to me and sat down by me on my right, as you say. When Dionysodorus and Euthydemus saw him, first of all they stopped and began talking to each other, looking now and then at us—for I watched them attentively—then they came and sat down, Euthydemus beside the lad, and the other beside me on my left; and the rest, anywhere they could. I then saluted the two as old acquaintances, and presently I said to Clinias, These gentlemen, Clinias, are Euthydemus and Dionysodorus, and they are both of them very

clever in great things, not little ones; they know
all about war, all that you ought to know if you
want to be a general—how to draw up your line
and to pitch your camp and to fight battles.
Besides, they can make you able to help yourself
in the law-courts when you are wronged.' These
remarks of mine they heard with contempt; at
least they exchanged a look and laughed, and
Euthydemus said, 'No, Socrates, we do not make
these subjects our serious business any more;
they are only our pastimes.' I answered with
surprise, 'Your business must be something very
fine, if you can treat such important matters as
pastimes: tell me, I entreat you, what it is—it
must be grand indeed.' 'Virtue,' he said, 'virtue,
Socrates, is what we consider ourselves able to
impart, better and more quickly than any one in
the world.'"

Most of the ensuing dialogue is a practical
reductio ad absurdum of what we call sophistry,
a series of word tricks and *tours de force* whereby
Euthydemus and Dionysodorus prove that black
is white—or any other colour they please. First of
all they propose to exercise their skill on the boy
Clinias, using the dialectic or question-and-answer
method, just as Socrates himself always does

—whereby one may infer that this form of argumentation is not peculiarly " Socratic," but rather the common property of contemporary teaching.

"So Euthydemus began something in this wise : ' Clinias, is it the wise men or the ignorant who learn ?' This was a serious question, and the boy blushed and looked to me. I saw that he was confused, and said to him, ' Courage, Clinias, and whichever you think the right answer give it like a man ; for it may be that this gentleman is doing you the greatest possible service.' Meanwhile Dionysodorus whispered into my ear, ' I tell you beforehand, Socrates, that whichever answer he gives, he will be proved wrong.'" So Clinias gives his answer, and of course is successfully contradicted, amid great applause from the attendant pupils, who sit there apparently in open-mouthed admiration of their teachers' cleverness. ' It is the wise who learn,' says Clinias. ' No,' replies Euthydemus, ' you learn when you do not know ; therefore you are ignorant when you learn, therefore you are not wise.' Then before Clinias can recover, Dionysodorus takes up the foil : ' But is it the wise boys who learn from dictation or the ignorant ?' ' Why, the wise of course.' ' So then it *is* the wise after all who learn '"—and

so on. The arguments are neither worse nor
better than the school-boy syllogism : Nothing is
better than a good conscience : sixpence is better
than nothing : therefore sixpence is better than a
good conscience. One can only trust that Plato's
portrait is a caricature. However, Clinias bears
it all meekly enough ; but his friend Ctesippus
(being, as Socrates says, a rather violent person)
takes philosophy much too seriously, and resents
it very much when he is proved to wish for Clinias'
hurt. " Thurian stranger! were it not rude, I would
say to you, ' Be it on your own head!' (σοὶ εἰς
κεφαλήν, which is good Greek for ' You're another !')
Euthydemus is quite unmoved, and calmly proceeds
to enmesh Ctesippus himself in subtleties, till the
young man is provoked to retort by actual rudeness, much in the language of the stupid child to
the infant prodigy, " I can't play the piano, and I
can't speak French, but I *can* punch your head !"
At last Socrates has to interfere and pacify the
disputants, not once but several times, as Ctesippus' common-sense cannot be induced to accept
the sophists' paradoxes. Socrates' own immediate
purpose is to discuss with Clinias the question—
naturally following from Euthydemus' assertion
that he can teach virtue—" What is the science

of good living?" and this question he proposes
to the sophists, but can get nothing out of them
but more and more quips and cranks. There is
really nothing like them in serious literature but
some of Shakspeare's exaggerated caricatures of
the euphuistic precocities of his own day—some
of the dialogue in the *Two Gentlemen of Verona*
for instance. The sophists are represented as
shirking serious discussion, and making chance
expressions opportunities for the display of verbal
gymnastics—even descending to grammatical puns
of the most puerile and dullest description.

"What is fitting for every workman? Can you
tell me, who is the man for smith's work?" "Why,
a smith, of course." "And who is the man for killing and flaying, boiling and roasting?" "A cook."
"And the fitting treatment in the case of every one
is the right one, is it not?" "Certainly." "And
the cook is the fitting man for cutting up and flaying? (προσήκει τὸν μάγειρον κατακόπτειν καὶ ἐκδέρειν).
Did you agree to that or not?" "I did—but deal
gently with me." "Then if you cut up and flay
the cook, you will be treating him in the fitting
way!"

Socrates himself is made the victim of this
method, and after some ineffectual attempts to

introduce the element of reason into the dialogue
—which is not playing the game according to the
rules—he is complaisant enough to let the professors prove to him that every one knows everything:
a paradox which Ctesippus takes too much *au
serieux*, and treats with some brutality; but which
Socrates himself accepts with feigned admiration
of its cleverness.

"These" (says Socrates to his friend Crito, to
whom he relates the encounter) "are clearly the
teachers for you and me." "Why," replies Crito,
"I met a man just now who had heard the whole
conversation and was completely disgusted by it
all. If *this* is philosophy, ought it to be taught to
our sons?" At last Socrates is serious. "Philosophy," he says, "must not be judged by the ways
of her exponents. Care nothing for the teachers
of philosophy, but test the thing itself; and if it
appears to you to be as I think it is, then pursue and practise philosophy, yourself and your
children."

If Gorgias and Protagoras are types of the most
respectable teachers of Socrates' day,—and even
they are treated without reverence,—their com-
parative excellence is strongly contrasted with the

shallowness and sophistry of two who may be taken as representing what, in Plato's view, was the charlatanism and quackery of the day—Euthydemus and Thrasymachus.

Not that these two figures are the least alike. Euthydemus (with his brother Dionysodorus) is really the prototype of Juvenal's "hungry Greekling"—

Grammaticus rhetor geometres pictor aliptes
Augur schoenobates medicus magus—

a versatile Jack-of-all-trades who is ready to teach any art or science, and who happens at the present moment to find what he calls "philosophy" the best paying speculation. But with him it is all a matter of verbal conceits and frivolous quibbles,— so hopelessly frivolous that Socrates does not consider him worth serious argument. For such there is no repentance. Thrasymachus is a very different person. In his way, he too is a representative of the worst teaching possible ; but the way is not that of Euthydemus. His name is not unknown to the intellectual history of the time ; he was a native of Chalcedon, an eloquent speaker, and a known teacher of rhetoric. In the *Phaedrus* Socrates alludes to his great power of exciting pity and anger in the minds of his hearers, and of

making and refuting calumnious accusations. In
the *Republic*, where he is most prominent, inter-
vening in the midst of Socrates' speculations on
the nature of justice, he is put forward as the
champion of the doctrine that Might is Right—
Justice the interest of the stronger. Perhaps this
may have been actually the tenor of some of his
teaching; or perhaps his manner was really as
cynical and hectoring as Plato represents it, and
thus made him a proper mouthpiece for the enun-
ciation of a cynical and brutal theory. There is
indeed hardly a less attractive portrait in Plato's
gallery than that of Thrasymachus. He is a man
possessed with a single idea, without tolerance for
any one who differs from him ; a blustering, bull-
headed arguer, trying—like Polus in the *Gorgias*—
to ride roughshod over all opposition, and coming
to grief himself in the attempt. His violence forms
an excellent foil to the gentle irony and affectation
of extreme timidity which is Socrates' most effective weapon in dealing with so brutal an opponent.
Yet he carries heavier guns than Euthydemus ;
he is worth serious argument; and eventually he
allows himself to be convinced into a kind of sulky
acquiescence. In spite of his rudeness and narrow-
ness, and even the greediness of money with which

Plato charges him, he is not wholly without a
redeeming feature ; on the whole, we part from
Thrasymachus on comparatively friendly terms.
He is a bully no doubt, and a stupid one, yet at
least he has a conviction.

"Now Thrasymachus had often tried to interrupt
our conversation, but had been always stopped by
the company, as they wished to hear the discussion
out.   But when we paused, and I had spoken as I
have said, he could not keep quiet any longer, but
leapt upon us like a wild beast crouching for the
spring, to tear us to pieces : Polemarchus and I
cowered before him in terror.   Addressing himself
to us all, he said, 'You have all been talking nonsense.   Why do you go on making these silly
concessions to each other ?   If you, Socrates, want
to know what justice really is, do not only ask
questions, and be so eager to find fault with the
answer, because you know that it is easier to ask
a question than to answer it : be the answerer
yourself, and tell me how you define justice.   And
mind you don't tell me that it is what is necessary,
or useful, or advantageous, or gainful, or profitable :
let us have your meaning plainly and exactly ex-
pressed ; I will stand no such nonsense as that
from you.'   At this I was clean dumfounded : it

terrified me to look at him. I really think that
if I had not seen him before he saw me I should
have lost my speech. As it was, when he was
beginning to get angered by the discussion, I had
the first look at him, so that I was able to answer.
'Thrasymachus,' I said timidly, 'do not be hard
on us ; any error that I or my friend make in discussing these questions is, you may be sure, quite
involuntary. Were it gold that we were seeking,
you know that we should never voluntarily baffle
the search by making concessions to each other ;
so you must not suppose that when the object of
our search is justice—a thing more valuable than
a great deal of gold—we would be so foolish as to
give in to each other, and not make every possible
effort to discover it. You must never think that !
No, the fact is that we have not the power to find
what we seek ; so clever people like you ought to
regard us with much more pity than anger.'

"To this he replied with a very bitter sardonic
grin : 'Why here is our old friend the irony of
Socrates again ! I knew it, and I told our friends
here, that you would never answer, but would pre-
tend ignorance and do anything rather than reply
to a question.' 'That,' said I, 'is because you are
so clever, Thrasymachus. Then you must also

H

have known that if you asked a friend to tell you how much makes twelve, with the warning that he was by no means to answer twice six, or three times four, or six times two, or four times three, because you would stand no such nonsense from him—it must, I say, have been clear to you that under such conditions you would get no answer. But suppose he had replied, " Why, Thrasymachus, you cannot surely mean that I am to give you no such answer as you describe, even if it be true, but that I am to depart from the truth," how would you have met him then ?' 'Well,' said he, 'and if I could not? the cases are not in the least alike.' 'I see nothing,' said I, 'against it. But never mind ; if, although there is really no parallel, the person questioned believes that there is, do you imagine that any prohibition of ours will prevent his answering according to his belief?' 'Is that then what you are going to do?' said he. 'Are you going to give me some one of the answers which I have forbidden?' 'Possibly I may,' I replied, ' if I approve of it on due consideration.' 'Well,' he said, 'if I show you another answer about justice, other and better than all those which we have heard, what penalty do you consent to pay?' 'The proper penalty of ignorance,' said I ;

'which is, to be instructed by knowledge. To that penalty I consent.' 'Very kind of you,' he retorted. 'But besides being taught, you must pay money down.' 'Certainly,' I said, 'when I get any.' 'Nay, you have it,' Glaucon put in; 'don't let that prevent your talking, Thrasymachus: we will all contribute for Socrates.' 'Ay, of course,' replied Thrasymachus, 'that Socrates may follow his old practice of not answering himself, but picking holes in some one else's replies.' 'Nay, my dear sir,' I said, 'one can hardly answer if in the first place he neither knows nor pretends to know, and in the second place is forbidden by a person so distinguished as yourself to state even any opinions which he may happen to entertain. It is you who ought to speak: you say that you know and have something to say.'"

Thrasymachus is the worst-tempered of all Socrates' opponents. He is led or rather dragged through an argument intended to refute his baldly-stated theory that justice is the interest of the stronger; and every now and then his ill-humour vents itself in abuse of his conqueror. Socrates is a "knavish disputant," "a dishonest quibbler." "You ought to have a nurse to stop your drivelling," —this, when Thrasymachus is obviously getting

the worst of it in argument. Presently he delivers
himself of a long and angry harangue to illustrate
his own peculiar doctrine; after which he is with
difficulty persuaded to stay and hear Socrates'
reply. Eventually he is so handled by the terrible
Socratic method, that he cannot possibly refuse to
give some kind of assent to the refutation of his
own theory—grudgingly enough. Instead of the
willing "Certainly" of most of Socrates' interlocutors, Thrasymachus' reply is generally "Perhaps"
and "Apparently." But at last he is convinced into
a kind of acquiescence in the conclusion that injustice can never be really profitable.

"You must not suppose that Thrasymachus'
assent to all this was given with as little trouble
as it takes to relate his words: it was extorted
from him much against his will, at the cost of a
great deal of perspiration, the weather being warm.
Indeed that was the first time that I ever saw
Thrasymachus blush. However, when we had
agreed that justice meant goodness and wisdom,
and injustice vice and ignorance, I continued:
'Well then, let us consider this settled, and come
to what we said about injustice being strong. Do
you not remember, Thrasymachus?' 'Yes,' he
said, 'I remember; but for my own part I am no

more satisfied than before with your conclusions,
and I have something to say about them. Were
I to say it, I know very well that you would call
me a stump orator. Either let me speak my mind,
or question me, if you like ; and I will say " very
well " and nod or shake my head, as one does when
listening to old wives' fables.' 'Nay,' I replied,
' do not answer what is contrary to your own
opinion.' ' Oh,' he answered, 'it is to please you,
since you will not let me speak. After all, what
else do you want?' 'Nothing indeed,' said I.
' Do so, if you must: I will put the questions.'
' Well, go on.' ' Let us then consider the succes-
sive steps of the discussion. I ask you my former
question, What is the relation of justice to injustice ?
It was stated that injustice was a more able and
powerful thing than justice ; but as it is, if justice
be wisdom and goodness, then of course it can
easily be shown to be also a stronger thing than
injustice, since injustice is ignorance. That must
now be clear to every one. However, I do not
wish to consider the question in the abstract :
take rather a concrete instance : would you call it
unjust for a city to attempt and succeed in the en-
slaving of other cities unjustly, and to keep many
as her enslaved subjects ?' 'Certainly I should,' he

replied. 'And that is what the best city, as being also most perfectly unjust, will be especially likely to do.' 'I understand,' said I, 'that such was your theory. But what I am considering about it is this: will the city that establishes a supremacy over another have its power without justice, or is justice a necessary concomitant?' 'If your recent definition is true,' he replied, 'and justice is wisdom, then the supremacy implies justice; but if mine is right justice is not necessary.' 'I am much obliged to you, Thrasymachus,' I observed, 'for not merely nodding and shaking your head, but giving me such excellent answers.' 'Oh,' he said, 'it is all to please you.'"

The preceding extracts may help to throw some light on the situations implied in some of Plato's dialogues. In those conversations, Socrates is not invariably the nominal protagonist. He is not represented as the idol of a clique. He does not "give his little senate laws" like Addison, nor is he always the king of his company like Dr. Johnson. It is not even his friends who are alone present or take a leading part: in fact very often it is his irreconcilable enemies: the teaching of Socrates is developed in encounter with the Scribes and Pharisees, and addressed to them quite as much as to his friends and sympathisers. Plato's object was undoubtedly to dramatise the collision of current opinions with each other and with the higher teaching of the greatest thinkers ; and for this purpose he could not have been better served than by the personality of Socrates, whose method was based on an affectation of ignorance, and whose main strength, as he himself said, lay even more in the eliciting of other men's thought than in the statement of his own.

CHAPTER VI

SOCRATES AMONG THE YOUNG : LYSIS AND CHARMIDES

IN the *Lysis* we have a momentary glimpse of the interior of an Athenian school—one, no doubt, of many which must have existed at the period ; but school life at Athens is a subject on which full knowledge is still to seek. Nothing emerges as to the schoolmaster's profession. No tradition has survived of Arnolds and Keates beneath the shadow of the Acropolis ; only here and there it is to be gathered from a passage in Plato or Aristophanes that the school was (as might be expected in an age of many-sided development) as important a factor in the intellectual life of the day as the lecture-room of the sophist ; which in fact corresponded to the University. Granted that there never was a period when the acquisition of knowledge was equally esteemed as a necessary foundation for success in life, and that the conditions of

Attic life put "home training" practically out of
the question, the establishment of schools, probably
large day-schools, was a necessity. And so we
find in the *Protagoras* a sketch of the education
in vogue—

"Teaching and advice begin in early childhood
and continue through life. As soon as ever a
child can understand what is said to him, his
nurse, his mother, his attendant, nay, his father
himself, begin to vie with each other in their efforts
for his improvement; every word and act is an
occasion for instruction by precept and example:
this (he is told) is just, that is unjust; this is fair,
that is ugly; this is right, that is wrong; do this,
do not do that. Perhaps he is willing to obey;
otherwise they keep him straight as if he were a
piece of wood growing warped and crooked, using
threats and blows. Presently he is sent to school,
where his masters are much more stringently enjoined to instruct him in good behaviour than in
writing and music. This charge is carried out;
and as soon as the boy has learnt his letters, and
is in a fair way to understand written compositions
as well as he previously learnt the meaning of
spoken words, his masters set the best poetry
before him on the desk for him to read and learn

by heart; this contains much sage advice, and many tales and eulogies of ancient heroes, who are intended as objects for the pupil to emulate and as models for his imitation. Similarly the music-masters are careful to instruct him in steadiness and good behaviour. Then, when he has learnt to play the lyre, they teach him more good poetry—lyric this time—set to the notes of the instrument; and they endeavour to attune the boy's mind to the various kinds of rhythm and harmony, thinking thereby to make him less rough and rude, and more useful in speech and action by being fulfilled with that perfection of rhythm and harmony which is necessary in all relations of life. Besides all this, the boy is sent to a trainer, so that with his body in a sound condition he may be the better able to obey the dictates of a good will, and may not be compelled by physical incapacity to shrink from danger in battle or elsewhere.

"Such is the practice of those who are best able to carry it out, that is, of the rich; it is their sons whose school education begins earliest and is the last to leave off."

So Aristophanes (in the *Clouds*) contrasts the old system of education and its old-fashioned sim-

plicity and strict regulations as to behaviour and
deportment, with the new-fangled methods of
latter-day instructors, who (he says) allow their
pupils far too much liberty, and make them both
effeminate and impertinent ; and Xenophon is probably describing what he considers to be the ideal
training for boys when he enlarges on the *régime*
instituted for the Spartan youth by Lycurgus :
how they were taught to look straight before them,
and never to speak as they walked ; so that (he
concludes) you would think they were more modest
than any young maidens.

From such references to Greek education it is
to be gathered that the Attic boy was in all
probability "supervised" to an extent which his
English successor would consider as only befitting
the other sex. Greek antiquity held such super-
vision to be an absolute necessity : the freedom
and autonomy of a modern public school were unknown : the training of an Attic boy is spoken of
as we now should describe the *régime* of a young
ladies' academy. Boys were escorted to school by a
slave who played the part of a chaperon or duenna,
and whose functions, even in playhours, seem to have
corresponded to those of the French *pion*. (Probably every school-boy knows that his head-master

has inherited a title originally belonging to a household slave who really had as little to do with education as a footman.) Protagoras speaks of the far greater stress laid by parents on "deportment" than on letters or music.

To us, save in the case of very small boys, such a system is unfamiliar: nor are we more familiar with the type of boy presented to us in the *Lysis*. Perhaps Plato's scholar is idealised; however that be, the character of the average English boy —temporarily brutalised by athletics and the unrestrained barbarity which till lately at least was the atmosphere of a public school—presents little similarity to the almost girlish grace, the combined simplicity and readiness of expression, of the Platonic fourth-form boy. Each age and each country has its own system, which is the best one for it. And there is no denying that the Lysis of Plato, drawn from life or not, is a wholly charming portrait.

"I was on my way," said Socrates, "from the Academy to the Lyceum, by the outer road just under the wall; and as I was going past the postern where the Panopus spring rises I met with Hippothales and Ctesippus, and a group of some other youths. As I came up Hippothales

saw me and said, 'Socrates, whither and whence
are you going?' 'I am going,' I said, 'from the
Academy straight to the Lyceum.' 'Well,' he
replied, 'just come straight here to us. Will you
not join? nay, 'tis worth your while.' 'Whither,'
I asked, 'do you mean? Who are your "you"?'
'This way,' he said, pointing to an enclosure with
an open door, opposite to the wall. 'That,' said
he, 'is where we spend our time, we and a great
many other excellent fellows.' 'Why, what is it?'
I asked. 'What is your occupation?' 'It is a
school lately built,' he said; 'and for our occupation, it is mostly discourse, in which we hope you
will share.' 'That is very kind of you,' I said.
'And who is the teacher here?' 'It is your friend,'
said he, 'and admirer, Miccus.' 'A good man too,'
said I, 'and an able teacher.' 'Will you follow us,'
said he, 'and see the students?'"

So, after some preliminary conversation, Socrates
joins the young men and they go into Miccus'
school, where a festival is apparently toward.

"Having come in" (the story goes on) "we
found that the boys had finished the sacrifice and
the offerings were nearly over, and they were all
in their best, playing knucklebones. Most of the
games were outside in the courtyard, but some

were in a corner of the vestibule, playing at odd
and even with knucklebones, which they took out
of baskets; while others stood and watched them.
Of these latter Lysis was one: he was standing
among the boys and youths, wearing a garland,
and conspicuous among all for the singular beauty,
and more than that for the singular nobility, of his
appearance. We walked over to the opposite side
of the room and sat down in a quiet place, where
we conversed. Lysis kept on turning round to
look at us, and evidently wanted to come nearer;
but for a time he hung back, too shy to come by
himself; till Menexenus came in from the court in
the middle of his play, and seeing Ctesippus and
me sat down beside us: on which Lysis followed
him and sat down by Menexenus.

"Turning to Menexenus I asked him, 'Son of
Demophon, which of you is the elder?' 'We have
not settled that,' said he. 'And I dare say you
differ as to which of you is the nobler,' I said.
'Certainly we do,' he replied. 'And so too as to
which is the handsomer?' They both smiled at
that. 'Well,' I said, 'I will not ask you which is
the wealthier, for you are friends—are you not?'
'Yes, indeed,' they said. 'Well, they say that
friends have all in common, so that, if you speak

truth about your friendship, here at least there is no difference between you.' To which they agreed.

"I was then proceeding to ask them which of the two were the juster and wiser. Before I could do so, some one came and called Menexenus away, saying the gymnastic teacher—who I believe was offering sacrifice—had sent for him. So after he was gone, I turned to Lysis: 'I suppose, Lysis,' said I, 'that your father and mother love you very much?' 'Certainly they do,' said he. 'Then of course they wish you to be as happy as possible.' 'Of course.' 'Now do you think that a man could be happy if he was a slave, and was not allowed to do anything he liked?' 'No, indeed, I do not,' said he. 'Well, then, if your father and mother love you and wish you to be happy, it is clear that they take great pains to make you happy.' 'Certainly they do,' he said. 'Do they then allow you to do what you like? can you do all that you wish without forbidding or hindrance from them?' 'Not I indeed, Socrates; most certainly they often hinder me.' 'How do you mean?' I said. 'When they wish you to be happy, do they prevent your doing whatever you wish?—or I will put it for you in this way. If you wished to take the reins and drive one of your

father's chariots in a race, would they not allow
you but prevent you?' 'Why, of course,' he said,
'they would not let me.' 'Well, whom would
they allow?' 'Oh, there is a chariot-driver paid by
my father.' 'Do you mean to say that they allow
a hireling rather than you to do what he pleases
with the horses, and pay him money for doing it
into the bargain?' 'Why, of course they do,' he
said. 'At least then, I suppose, they will let you
drive the cart, and even if you wanted to beat the
animals with the whip there would be no objection.'
'Indeed there would,' he said. 'What?' said I;
'may no one beat them?' 'Yes,' he said, 'the
carter.' 'Is he a slave or a freeman?' 'A slave.'
'It seems, then, that your parents think more of a
slave than of you, their own son, and will trust their
property to him rather than to you, and allow
him to do what he likes, while they forbid you.
And I will ask you another question. Do they let
you govern yourself, or will they not trust you
even here?' 'Of course,' he said, 'they do not
trust me.' 'Well, who does govern you?' 'There
he is,' he said; 'the children's attendant.' 'Is he a
slave?' 'Assuredly he belongs to us.' 'That is
hard indeed,' I said, 'that you who are free
should be governed by a slave.' 'And how does

the attendant govern you?' 'I suppose,' he said,
'by taking me to school.' 'And are you governed
there too, by your teachers?' 'Certainly.' 'It seems
that your father willingly sets over you a great
many masters and governors. Well, when you go
home to your mother, does she, in order to see you
happy, allow you to do what you like with her
wool or her loom, when she is weaving?—for I
presume she does not forbid you to handle her
comb or her shuttle or any other part of the
spinning gear.' At this Lysis laughed, and said,
'Indeed, Socrates, not only does she forbid me, but
I should be beaten if I were to handle them.'"

The conclusion of the matter is, of course, that
knowledge brings power. "'Where we have
knowledge all will freely trust us to act,—Greeks,
aliens, men and women,—and in such things we
shall do what we please, and no one will wish to
hinder us, but we shall have full authority over
ourselves and over others : these things will be
ours, for we can draw advantage from them.
But in matters of which we have no knowledge we
shall never be allowed to act as we please, and all
will hinder us as far as they can, not only strangers,
but our parents and very closest relatives : in these
matters we shall be subject to others ; they will be

I

foreign to us, for we can draw no advantage from them. Do you agree that that is so?' 'I do.' 'Shall we then be loved and held dear by any one for matters in which we are useless?' 'No, indeed,' he said. 'So now no one can be loved by another—not even you by your father—for being useless.' 'It seems not,' he said. 'Then, my boy, if you get wisdom, all will hold you near and dear ; for you will then be useful and good : otherwise no one will love you, neither your parents, nor your near kin, nor any one else.

" ' Now is it possible, Lysis, to be proud of things which we do not know?' 'It cannot be,' he said. 'And if you need a teacher, you cannot yet have knowledge.' 'That is true.' 'Then if you have no mind at all as yet, you cannot have a high mind.' 'Apparently not, Socrates.'

*   *   *   *   *

"With that Menexenus came back and sat down in his old place by Lysis. Then Lysis whispered to me in a very boyish, loving way—not loud enough for Menexenus to hear—'Tell Menexenus too, Socrates, what you have told me.' I said, 'You shall tell him yourself, Lysis ; for I know you have listened attentively.' 'Certainly I have,' he said."

The above extracts are taken from the introductory chapters of the dialogue called *Lysis*, and only serve as a preface to the real argument, which deals with the true basis of friendship. I have quoted from them rather than from later parts of the dialogue, because it seems to me that it is in such introductions that the personal relation of Socrates to his interlocutors is best revealed. By these more than by what we may call the doctrinal chapters one can in some sort begin to realise as well the social charm of Socrates, as the kind of persons with whom he was accustomed to converse, and the kind of situation which forms the setting to his conversation.

The *Lysis* is a "talk" on friendship; and as in most real talks—and therefore as in many of Plato's dialogues—the main question is not really settled one way or the other. Socrates' last word is, "If friendship is neither this nor that" (and he enumerates different possibilities) "then ἐγὼ μὲν οὐκέτι ἔχω τί λέγω": "behold, we know not anything."

"Having said this, I was minded to question some one of the elder men. But then came Menexenus' and Lysis' attendants, like evil spirits; they had the boys' brothers with them, and kept

urging our friends to come home, for it was late
by this time. At first we and the bystanders tried
to get rid of them ; but they cared nothing for us,
and went on calling the boys, speaking angrily
with their foreign accent. Apparently they had
drunk too much at the Hermaea, and it was impossible to make anything of them ; so we yielded
to them and broke up the conference. However,
as they were just about going, I said to Lysis
and Menexenus : 'Now we have made ourselves
ridiculous, you and I, for all my old age. Our
friends will say as they go home that we fancy
ourselves to be friends (you see I consider myself
one of you), yet what a friend really is we have not
been able to discover ! ' "

In the dialogue called *Charmides*, the title-rôle
is played by a youth who is receiving the homage
which we reserve for female beauty. To us, beauty
in a man is a matter of small importance. But in
Hellas different ideas prevailed : on Socrates'
return from the campaign of Potidaea all the talk
is of the rising generation of youths ; the girls
who would now be the reigning belles of a small
town are simply left out of account altogether in
Plato. All the attention and admiration is for

their brothers. It was they and not the Attic
damsels whom Phidias chose to represent as the
types of the highest human grace; nay, even the
conventional presentation of Athena has far more
the beauty of a man than of a maid. Of this
Attic grace Charmides is a perfect example. He,
like Alcibiades, is "the mould of form" of young
Athens. "All gazed at him," says Socrates, "as
at a statue." Moreover, he is not only perfectly
beautiful: he is highborn—a descendant of one of
those old families which Athens, for all her democratic institutions, still especially delighted to
honour; and while he is thus like enough to Alcibiades in all else, he has that which Alcibiades
lacked, the saving grace of σωφροσύνη or steadiness,
so especially necessary to an Athenian stripling.

Here, as in the *Lysis*, the Platonic Socrates is
a picture of the philosopher paying philosophic
homage to an outward beauty which, if it is to be
perfect, must be accompanied by a corresponding
perfection of the mind within. After his first
bewilderment at sight of the noble grace of Charmides, his demeanour to the young man is instinct
with that kind wisdom (made earnest by the deep
reverence of mature age for the bright actuality
and brighter possibilities of youth), which is the

distinguishing characteristic of all Socrates' intercourse with the young.

"Now when Critias heard this from me" (Socrates had offered to cure Charmides of a headache
by a method involving mental as well as physical
treatment), "he said, 'My young kinsman's headache will indeed have been a stroke of luck for
him, if the cure of his head implies of necessity an
improvement of his mind. However, I can tell
you that Charmides has been thought to surpass
his compeers not only in outward beauty, but in
that gift which you say you have a charm to
confer ; that is, steadiness. Is not that so?' 'Certainly,' I said. 'Be well assured then,' he replied,
'that he is considered by far the steadiest of the
rising generation, being as he is up to his present
age no whit inferior to any one in any other
respect.' 'Well,' said I, 'and it is but right too
that you should be conspicuous for all that is
good, Charmides ; for I suppose none of the
present company would readily point to two
Athenian houses whose union should naturally
produce a fairer and better offspring than did the
union of your parents' families. The praises of
your father's house—Critias' and Dropidas' before
him—have come down to us from the poems of

Solon, Anacreon, and many others, all telling us of
its excellence in beauty and virtue, and whatever else is esteemed as prosperity. Nor is your
mother's family less celebrated; wherever your
mother's brother Pyrilampes was ambassador, at
the court of the Great King or any Asiatic potentate, he was held, they say, to be as proper a man
as any in the king's dominions; and altogether
that side of your family is not inferior to your
father's. Such being your parentage, it is to be
expected that you should always take the first
place. In outward seeming, dear son of Glaucon,
you are like to bring no discredit on your lineage;
and if, as your cousin says, nature has given you a
sufficient share of steadiness and the other virtues,
you are indeed a fortunate son of your mother.
However, this is how the case stands: if what
Critias says is true,—if you have already steadiness, and are sufficiently steady,—you have then
no need of the charm either of Zamolxis or the
Hyperborean Abaris, but may at once receive by
itself the drug to cure your head; but if it seems
that you still lack that virtue, we must use the
incantation upon you before the drug. I will ask
you, then, to tell me for yourself: do you assent
to what Critias says? can you say that you pos-

sess sufficient steadiness already, or do you need more?'

"At this Charmides blushed, and looked the handsomer for it; for his modesty became his youth. Then he gave me a very worthy answer: it was not easy, he replied, to say yes or no at once to my question. 'Suppose I confess that I am not steady, I shall be accusing myself in a very unnatural way, besides giving the lie to Critias here and many others, who give me credit, as he says, for steadiness; while if I say that I am, self-praise will perhaps give offence. So that I really have no answer to give.' I replied, 'What you say, Charmides, is quite right. It seems to me,' I continued, 'that we must help each other to examine the question whether you have or not that of which I ask: thus *you* will not be obliged to give an answer which you dislike, and *I* shall not undertake the case without a proper diagnosis. So if you consent, I will examine the matter with your assistance; or if not, we will let it be.' 'Nay,' he said, 'I consent most willingly: you have my full permission to conduct your examination as you think best.'"

As the *Lysis* leads to no formal definition of friendship, so the *Charmides* leads to no formal conclusion about σωφροσύνη. We construct our best definition of it (says Socrates), and then are met by tyrannous logic, which will not prove steadiness to be useful. At this Socrates is ironically distressed, more, as he says, on Charmides' account than his own: "Yet I cannot believe," he continues, "that this is really so, and that σωφροσύνη is useless. Rather I think that I am a poor seeker, and that steadiness is a great good, which if you possess, you are supremely blest."

CHAPTER VII

THE 'SYMPOSIUM'

BOTH Plato and Xenophon have left a picture of Socrates in convivial society. Xenophon's *Symposium* or " Drinking-Bout " is the simpler, the more naïve, and probably the truer sketch of the two ; but it is not free from a certain Spartan or even Roman grossness which is quite absent in the Platonic version. In both, Socrates is an intentionally rather grotesque figure ; but the grotesqueness of the " Silenus-like " figure is less apparent as presented by the art of Plato, whose whole description is moulded by that exquisite sense of fitness which is the property of all truly Athenian genius. One sees how differently the same theme may be treated by a most meritorious *littérateur* like Xenophon, and by a genuinely poetic imagination. Plato's guests move in an atmosphere of sweetness and light. His incomparable skill and " lightness of touch " inform the whole situation with an inevitable reality, however abrupt the contrasts with which it is chequered : so that high philosophical disquisition seems perfectly proper to the *abandon* of an Athenian dinner-table, and after Socrates has reached the loftiest heights of the ideal it does not—somehow—in the least jar the reader's sensibilities to be confronted with the real in the shape of a drunken libertine's confession of his amours—truly a heavy demand to make, even on the Greek language and the genius of Plato. In the whole dialogue the serious alternates with the comic, and Socrates' portrait is also serio-comic : his irony takes the form of an eccentric humour which does not in the least obscure but rather enhances his greatness.

The *Symposium* is a description of an Athenian supper-party : all the guests are men. It is worth remarking, by the way, that the part played by ladies in Athenian society is to the last degree unimportant. They no longer exercise the duty of hostess : the great ladies of the Homeric poems —a Helen or an Arete, who sits at her husband's board and talks freely to his guests—have given place to the household drudge, whose highest merit is " not to be spoken of." In the fifth century B.C. a man's domestic life—except in a few instances, such as that of Socrates himself, who was married to a notorious shrew—has practically ceased to make part of his biography. It is a thing not worth mentioning. A wife is a necessary evil—necessary perhaps, an evil certainly. Plato's communistic theory abolishes even the *Hausfrau:* women are to form a State harem, and to play no other part. Aristophanes' women are either nonentities, or only prominent in order to be ridiculous. As for Socrates, apart from one or two reported or imagined conversations between him and certain ladies whose interests were in no sense domestic,—and women of this class alone appear to have exercised some influence in the Hellas of that day,—his attitude towards the fair sex is that of the Athenians of his time—contemptuous toleration.

The scene of the Platonic Banquet is the house of the poet Agathon—described after his death by Aristophanes in the *Frogs* as " a good poet, and one regretted by his friends "—who is entertaining a select circle of acquaintances the day after his first tragedy has won the prize in the theatre. Socrates has come without special invitation, and in fact almost accidentally ; but he is none the less a welcome guest. After dinner, it becomes a question how to spend the evening—in other words, whether to get drunk or not. It appears that all the company are glad of an excuse for sobriety: some are naturally temperate, others have drunk deep the night before, and would fain keep sober now. Eventually it is agreed that no one shall take more wine than he likes; that the flute-girl— engaged by Agathon as an indispensable accessory to every gentleman's dinner-table—shall be sent away to play to herself or in the drawing-room (ταῖς γυναιξὶ ταῖς ἔνδον, "to the women within"); and that the evening shall be devoted (think of it, O dinner-givers of the nineteenth century!) to the delivery of a series of set speeches, each in turn celebrating the powers of Love. Each of the guests is to bear his part in dwelling on that aspect of the passion which appeals to him most strongly. Thus the *Symposium* is the "locus classicus" on Love as regarded by the ancients, before other conceptions and other ideals had been created by religion and romance: it is a summary of the best that can be said upon the subject. Every speaker has his point of view to emphasise and adorn. To one Love is a matter of political expediency—the true lover will be the best and most energetic citizen. Agathon's theme is the

poets' and painters' Eros; Sophocles' "Love invincible, Love that nightly haunts a maiden's soft
cheek." Another draws the distinction (for which
perhaps we give antiquity too little credit) between
Ἀφροδίτη πάνδημος and Ἀφροδίτη οὐρανία, the lower
passion and the higher sentiment—while again the
heavenly Aphrodite is the "one spirit" whose

"plastic stress
Sweeps through the dull dense world."

Aristophanes has a quaint conceit that the Creator
of the world doubled the number of its inhabitants
by dividing each living being in half, and that Love
is our natural attraction to that other half which
is necessary to complete our existence.

Socrates, as usual, has the last word. His
contribution to the theme is that of one who is
by his own assertion a professor of the art of Love,
and a former student in the school of a lady "in
the lore of love deep learned to the red heart's
core," one Diotima of Mantinea. Love is to him
not only the desire for one's other half, as in the
jesting apologue of Aristophanes, nor the bright
creature of Agathon's fancy; it is—to those who
can understand and know—that instinct which,
taught and purified, becomes at last the desire for
not only beautiful things but the Beautiful itself,

αὐτὸ τὸ καλόν, the abstract ideal apart from concrete presentations. "This be my praise of love—or call it what you will." Love—even when many degrees removed from mere carnal desire, still love of the individual—is for others to praise: it remains for Socrates to endow the original sensual instinct with a capacity for development into the highest and noblest of all desires. To him Love is in the highest sense the "fulfilling of the law."

To interrupt the discourse when it has reached its highest level by the introduction of a drunken reveller, would for a worse artist than Plato be to take the step from the sublime to the ridiculous. Just as Socrates has finished speaking a great noise is heard without, and presently Alcibiades enters, very drunk, and calling loudly for Agathon, whom, he says, he has come to crown in honour of his dramatic victory. It is pointed out to him that if he is to join the company he must conform to the rules of the evening, and take his turn in saying something in praise of Love. "What? praise any one but Socrates in his presence?" "Well then," says Eryximachus, "praise Socrates."

The *Symposium*, as I have said, is a dialogue of carefully-calculated contrasts. Nothing could be more effective than the antithesis between the subject and the speaker of Alcibiades' encomium ; nothing could more vividly present the striking individuality of Socrates than its illustration by one who regards it primarily as mere "strangeness," ἀτοπία,—a Greek of the Greeks, an Athenian of the Athenians, the very type of the Attic ἀνειμένη δίαιτα or lack of restraint,—nay more, an Athenian drunk: for Alcibiades has arrived at the confidential and expansive stage of intoxication, and is evidently in a mood to tell the company what he really thinks of his master.

The Socrates of the *Symposium*, half humorously and half reverently drawn by Alcibiades, is not an unfamiliar portrait. It is the vivid and concrete presentation of that character which is elsewhere inferred from his teaching or described by his biographers. It is Socrates practising what he preaches,—continent himself, as he ever asserts the necessity of continence for others ; contemptuous of physical comfort and bearing hardship lightly: just as in the *Phaedo*, for instance, he speaks of the body as a mere encumbrance (and fortunately perhaps for his consistency, Socrates possessed a frame of iron capable of defying any discomfort); courageous in face of the enemy, just

as he had the courage to vote for the acquittal of
those generals whom Athenian public opinion was
making the scapegoats of a humiliating defeat,
just as the *Apology, Crito,* and *Phaedo* show him
courageous in face of death by the hands of the
executioner.   What then, asks Juvenal, at the
close of his Tenth Satire, shall men pray for?
For this only—a courage that has no fear of
death, that counts length of days least among
nature's gifts, that can bear any toil, that knows
no anger nor desire, and prefers the sorrows
and labours of Heracles to the loves and the
luxuries of Sardanapalus.   Socrates is not far
removed from Juvenal's Stoic model.   At the
same time his stoicism, to speak anachronistic-
ally, is human and natural, untinged with the
"Nirvana" of freedom alike from anger and
desire.   But to Alcibiades he is simply and frankly
incomprehensible ; and this probably represents
the attitude of the average Athenian : only it was
unfortunate for Socrates that the general run of
men regard incomprehensibility as criminal.

After a series of anecdotes illustrating Socrates'
capacity for bearing hardship, and his contempt of
danger,—how he can drink without getting drunk,
and yet at the same time does not care for drink-

ing,—how he saved Alcibiades' life at the battle of
Delium, and in the general rout that followed
walked quietly along as if he had been in the streets
of Athens βρενθυόμενος καὶ τὠφθαλμὼ παραβάλλων,
according to the phrase of Aristophanes, " with his
nose in the air, and looking from side to side,"
viewing friends and enemies with equal uncon-
cern,—after describing Socrates' bearing as a
soldier, his encomiast concludes: " Such stories
might perhaps be related about another man. But
what is really most wonderful is that he is so
unlike everybody else, of all that live or ever have
lived ! For instance, you might very well compare
Brasidas or Pericles to Achilles or Nestor, or other
heroes of antiquity; but here is one who is com-
parable to no one at all except it be to a Silenus
or a Satyr. Just so his discourses at first sight
appear simply ridiculous; but when you open them
and really examine them closely, you find that no
others are so divine or contain in themselves so
many pictures of virtue; they embrace, in fact, all
that he should look to who intends to lead a
blameless life " (τῷ μέλλοντι καλῷ κἀγαθῷ ἔσεσθαι).
Then Agathon is warned to be on his guard
against this extraordinary person, who will only
deceive him as he has deceived Alcibiades and

others with his ironical pretence of friendship. To all of which Socrates answers: "It is evident, Alcibiades, that you are not so drunk after all : you wrap up your meaning so skilfully. But it is quite clear to me that you are jealous, and want to make me and Agathon quarrel,"—whereupon follows a humorous wrangle as to which is to be privileged to sit next the host and hero of the evening ; ending, of course, in the victory of Socrates.

"So then," says Aristodemus, who is the narrator throughout, " Agathon rose, intending to sit next Socrates ; when suddenly a great number of revellers came to the street door, and finding it open, as some one was just going out, they entered and sat down with us, and there was a great clamour, and we were all compelled to drink a great deal of wine, without rule or order. Eryximachus and Phaedrus and some others took their departure ; I went to sleep, and as it was late at night, I slumbered soundly till I woke at cockcrow. The rest of the party were all asleep or gone, and only Agathon and Aristophanes and Socrates were awake — and there they were, sitting and drinking out of a large cup, passing it round from left to right. Socrates was talking to

the others. Most of what he said I do not remember ; for I had not heard the beginning of
the conversation, and was rather sleepy. But it
came to this, that Socrates was compelling them
to admit that the composition of tragedy and
comedy was the same man's work, and that the
true tragedian was really a comedian. As this
conclusion was being forced upon them (not,
indeed, that they exactly followed the argument),
first Aristophanes and then Agathon dropped off
to sleep, the latter as day was dawning. Having
thus laid them to rest, Socrates got up and went
away (I following him as usual) to the Lyceum,
bathed there, passed the day there according to
his wont, and having so spent it till evening, went
home to sleep."

The following is Agathon's poetical rhapsody
on the theme of Love—a picture unequalled in
Plato for sensuous grace and brilliancy of colour.

"Now for my part I will not say anything until
I have first said how I ought to say it. For it
seems to me that all who have hitherto spoken are
much less singing the praises of the god than con-
gratulating men on the blessings which they owe
to him : what is the nature of the giver himself no
one has told us : whereas you cannot praise any

one rightly unless you describe the subject of your speech as well as his works. That is the way for us to discuss Love now, to praise himself first for what he is, and then his gifts.

"This is what I maintain :—That while all the gods are blessed, Love—if I may say so without offence—is the blessedest of them all, because he is both the fairest of them and the best. How he is the fairest you will see from my description. To begin with, he is the youngest of the gods. His own action is the best proof of what I say; for he flees with speed from old age, which all know to be swift—swift enough, at least, to overtake us sooner than need be. Now Love abhors Age, and will not come even within a long way of him; but with the young he ever consorts and abides: it is a true old saying that like keeps company with like. So, although I agree with much that Phaedrus said, I cannot consent to his theory that Love is older than Cronos and Iapetos : rather I hold him to be the youngest of the gods, eternally young ; and granting the truth of Hesiod's and Parmenides' stories about troubles in heaven of old, I judge those troubles to have been produced not by Love but by Necessity. If Love had been there the gods would never have mutilated and

imprisoned and otherwise maltreated each other ;
no, it would have been all harmony and peace, as it
is now and has been ever since Love has been lord
of heaven. Well then, he is young, and delicate
moreover ; so much so that he needs a poet
like Homer to describe how soft and tender he
is. You know, Homer in describing Ate says she
is a goddess, and delicate—at least in the feet—

' Her feet they are full delicate ; for not on earth they fare,
But high above the heads of men she walketh in the air '—

an excellent illustration of delicacy : she is represented as walking not on a hard but on a soft
substance. I would employ this same illustration
to show that Love is delicate. For he does not
walk on earth—nor over men's skulls, which are
not at all soft—but walks and dwells in the softest
of all existing things : it is the natures and souls
of men and gods that he inhabits : not all souls
throughout : he is repelled by those that are hard
of nature, but such as are soft he chooses for his
dwelling. So then, as it is the softest of the soft
that comes in contact with his feet and every part
of him, he must needs be most delicate. Besides
his youth and delicateness, his frame is lithe and
supple ; for were he stark and stiff he could never

so wind himself about us, and be so unfelt through
all our being at his first coming and at his departure. That he is lithe and justly proportioned is
proved beyond doubt by that gracefulness which
all admit to be an attribute of Love; for Love and
uncouthness are ever at war. Beauteous too he is
of complexion, as is shown by his dwelling still
with bloom : Love stays not with aught withered
and faded, be it body or soul or what you will;
but all places of perfume and bloom are his chosen
resting-place and abode.

"Concerning the god's beauty much more might
be said, yet even this is sufficient; and now I will
proceed to speak of his goodness. Whereof this
is the highest praise, that Love neither wrongs god
nor man, nor is wronged by any; for when he sub-
mits, it is not to force (since that cannot touch
Love); nor does he use force, since all obedience
to Love is willing service, and the laws whereby
States are ruled declare that agreements made by
mutual consent are not wrongful but just. Just,
then, he is, and withal supremely temperate ; for all
admit that to be temperate is to rule our pleasures
and passions, and that no pleasure is greater than
Love ; but if pleasures are less than he they must
be ruled by him : so then Love rules pleasures and

passions, and thus must be pre-eminently temperate.
Moreover he is so brave, that even Ares cannot
withstand him : Ares is mastered by Love, the
love as it is said of Aphrodite : so as the master
is greater than his servant, and Love masters one
who is surpassingly brave, he must himself be the
very ideal of bravery. So much, then, for the god's
justice, temperance, and courage ; and now it remains to speak of his wisdom, which I will essay
to do as worthily as I may. First—for I give the
place of honour to my own art, as Eryximachus
did to his art of medicine—I maintain that Love
is so cunning a poet that he can even transmit
the gift to another; for every man, howe'er unapt
before, becomes a poet at the touch of Love. This
is a fitting proof that Love is in brief a skilful
maker of every kind of poetry ; for no one can
impart or teach to another what he does not himself possess or know. Moreover, it is past all doubt
that the making of all living things is the work
of Love's cunning wisdom ; for by this all things
have birth and growth. And we know too that
in the sphere of art craftsmen inspired by Love
attain to fame and renown, while those untouched
by him remain obscure. It was by the guidance
of desire and love that Apollo discovered the arts

of archery and medicine and divination, so that he too must be of Love's disciples; and the Muses and Hephaestus and Athena and Zeus were all schooled by the love of their several arts,—whether of song and story, or metallurgy, or weaving, or government. Thus it was that the troubles of the gods were composed by the birth of Love among them, by which we must certainly understand the love of beauty; for ugliness cannot be the object of Love. Before that, as I began by saying, it was the rule of Necessity that caused the gods all their grievous troubles; but as soon as this god was born, gods and men alike derived all blessings from their love of beautiful things.

"Thus, Phaedrus, I hold that it is by virtue of being himself already supreme in beauty and goodness that Love can bestow like gifts on others. Nay, I am even moved to attempt a couplet, and to say that it is he who

To men gives peace, and stills the raging deep,
And calms the boisterous winds, and lulls our cares to sleep.

"Love makes us void of estrangement and full of mutual affinity, causing us to assemble together in such wise as now: at holy feasts and dances and sacrifices he comes as our leader: he is a replenisher of courtesy, a banisher of boorishness; lavish of

good-will, chary of ill-will ; benign to the good, a
sight for wise men to behold and gods to admire ;
a treasure for those that lack it to covet, and those
that have it to cherish ; sire of softness and dainty
delights, grace, desire, longing ; caring for good,
caring not for evil ; in labour, in terror, in longing,
in converse the best of pilots, comrades, allies, and
preservers ; pride of heaven and earth : of all guides
fairest and best, whom every man should follow,
bearing well his part in that sweet song which
Love sings to charm the hearts of gods and men."

CHAPTER VIII

IT falls to the lot of few men to find two biographers among their personal friends. Not that either Plato or Xenophon is a biographer in the common sense of the word : rather they are both students of Socrates' character from different points of view. Each of them saw and has transmitted to us that manifestation of his master's mind which was most apparent to him ; and the two men were widely different, and thus saw Socrates with different eyes. To Plato, the ardent, imaginative, poetical thinker—to Plato the moralist and mystic in one, searching the secret ways of the universe and the heart of man—the speculative side of Socrates' thought was most familiar and most apparent. The dialogues of Plato represent Socrates' way of dealing with abstract ideas, and his attitude towards man in relation to these abstractions. Plato was a student. Xenophon,

on the other hand, was — not in the sense of
Callicles — a man of the world and a man of
action : perhaps the best specimen (in a moral
sense) of Athenian versatility. Nothing in the
world was without interest for him. He was a
capable general,—on one occasion even a brilliant
leader of men,—and a capable writer on a large
variety of subjects, always with a clear, practical
sense of the real and the necessary. To him
Socrates was primarily not the great thinker, but
the great moral teacher, the good influence in his
generation ; the *Memorabilia* is mainly a record of
the good that Socrates did, and a protest against
the calumny of those who accused him of corrupting
youth. Plato's view of his master is the poetical
vision : Xenophon's is the prosaic record. And
by this I do not for a moment imply that the
poetical view is less true than the other.

Xenophon was a man of action and adventure,
and he lived in troublous times. If, as seems prob-
able, he was born in 431 B.C., his birth coincided
in time with the opening of the long Peloponnesian
War. Of his youth and early manhood little or
nothing is known, nor have we any formal record
of his relations with Socrates. It seems to be
tolerably clear from the length of time to which

Xenophon's *Reminiscences* refer, that he must have met Socrates early in life and lived much in his society. He is not, however, a personage in the dialogues of his contemporary Plato. The death of Socrates occurred about the same time as, or immediately after, the episode in Xenophon's life on which his fame as a general rests. In 401 B.C. the young student—for up to this time he had apparently taken no active part in public life—was induced to join a force of Greeks whom Cyrus the Younger had engaged to assist him in maintaining his claim to the throne of Persia. The expedition failed of its object. Cyrus fell in battle, and the Greek generals were treacherously murdered. The lives of the whole Hellenic force were endangered, isolated as they were amidst enemies in an unknown country. Xenophon, by virtue of no official rank, but simply native energy and capacity, was constituted one of their leaders; and with him especially rests the credit of the memorable "Retreat of the Ten Thousand," through the wild mountains and wilder tribes of Armenia.

Xenophon returned to Greece in 399 B.C., to learn —with what indignant sorrow one may imagine —that his master had been put to death in the spring of that same year. Had the *Memorabilia*

been written at that time, probably it would have
been an angrier protest against his countrymen's
injustice.   As it was, fortune had other adventures
in store for Xenophon; and it was not till at least
twelve years later that he found time, while living
in retirement at Scillus, to put together his recollections of Socrates and his teaching.   The teaching
which a man recollects is that which finds an echo
in his own character ; and Xenophon, the philo-
Laconian, himself "cast in a Dorian mould," had
seen in Socrates mainly the master who inculcated
moral goodness and simplicity of life—who taught
the rule of righteousness, " but first he folwede it
himselve."   This, no doubt, was the guidance to
which Xenophon himself looked back with the
warmest gratitude and the clearest understanding.
And as Plato has impressed the stamp of his mind
on the Socrates of the dialogues, so it is natural
that Xenophon's own temperament has not only
selected from the discourses to which he listened
in youth, but has also considerably modified their
form, and in some cases added to them.

Xenophon has often been reproached with degrading the character and method of Socrates.
The principal figure in the *Memorabilia* is sometimes (it is asserted) platitudinous, and sometimes

merely frivolous ; and in short, had Socrates'
conversation been really such as Xenophon describes it, not only would the speaker have been
beaten and kicked (it appears from the chronicle of
Diogenes Laertius that the " Socratic method "
occasionally provoked not only the retort dis-
courteous but the *argumentum ad baculum*), but
the streets would have been emptied by the ap-
proach of so portentous a bore : an assumption
which is of course intolerable. It is clear, then
(say the critics), that this so-called memoir cannot
really deserve its name ; and moreover these numerous conversations which Xenophon professes to
report are far too long to have been remembered
verbatim. Hence we are presented with a choice
between two alternatives : either there is much
more Xenophon than Socrates in the *Memorabilia*
(it was the custom after Socrates' death to compose
more or less imaginative works purporting to be
about him, but really only using him as a mouthpiece for the writer's opinion, and Xenophon only
followed the fashion), or we may adopt the easy
and attractive plan of pronouncing a large part of
the *Memorabilia* spurious, the work of a late and
unskilful hand.

All this kind of criticism is based on the

assumption that a great man can only talk about great things in a great way—an assumption which daily experience disproves. Plato makes Socrates talk beautifully: yet even from Plato we gather that to the casual hearer his conversation was of common and even of vulgar things. In the *Symposium*, Alcibiades says of his master that his ordinary talk was about common men and common things, "donkeys and shoemakers and tanners"; so that to most the real and inner meaning was indiscernible. Now Xenophon was a plain man, and presumably had not the gift of insight into the real and higher signification which underlay the rude exterior of Socrates' daily talk; nor should *we* have known the "true inwardness" of that talk were it not that we have Plato for a guide. Plato has thoroughly understood, emphasised, and adorned the real purpose of Socrates— that is, the pursuit of knowledge. Xenophon is not unaware of that purpose : he says distinctly in one passage at least that the philosopher's main object was to arrive at the true signification of words and things—what is government and who is the true ruler, and so forth; but generally he has seen Socrates as he would appear to the ordinary man. Indeed, it is for the public of ordinary men that Xenophon is writing. His avowed object is to dwell on that aspect of Socrates in which he appears as a teacher " making for righteousness," as a beneficial and not a harmful influence in the State, not at all as a philosopher concerned with speculations which to many seemed' actively bad, and to most unprofitable at best. Xenophon's is that side of the great teacher which most strongly appealed to one who, like Xenophon, was mainly concerned with practical matters. Of course that painful subordination of objectivity to effect which characterises so much of ancient literature, and is so displeasing to modern zealots for so-called accuracy, is too notorious to allow us to assume that Xenophon never dramatises an opinion of his own ; but the hypothesis of " subjectivity " is least of all likely to be true precisely in those passages which give most offence to modern criticism. For instance—it is hardly possible that Xenophon could have thought it worth while seriously to record as Socratic those valuable counsels as to the right proportion of bread and meat at dinner, had the advice not been actually given. This kind of table-talk is natural enough to chronicle, but to suppose it invented would be to doubt the sanity of the inventor.

L

The same defence may be urged against that criticism which attributes as much of the *Memorabilia* as it does not agree with to the hand of an interpolator. Why any one should have taken the trouble to insert in a serious work chapters on dinner-table etiquette, is a problem which passes the understanding of man. But the theory of interpolation, which should be the last reserve of despairing criticism, is too often placed in the van of the attack.

Xenophon's position is in the main that of the simple-minded observer—"I," he says frankly, "am a mere layman," ἐγὼ δὲ ἰδιώτης εἰμί—recalling what he could of a philosopher's table-talk; and philosophers at home have not always talked for the world. That these utterances are in dialogue form does not prove that the biographer professes to report dialogues verbatim : it only shows that conversation, not monologue, was Socrates' method which is skilfully developed by Plato. Xenophon was neither a Plato to idealise, nor a Boswell to report. He had not Plato's gift of seizing and adorning the really differentiating and striking side of Socrates' method and character; nor had he the vivid shorthand-reporter's gift of a Boswell.

That very want of artistic arrangement which

characterises the *Memorabilia* is a mark of its genuineness. The whole work is devoid of ruling method and system, except in so far that the general purpose of the writer is manifest enough —to prove that Socrates, the condemned and executed criminal, was after all a useful member of society. " I have often wondered," says Xenophon on his first page, "why the Athenians put Socrates to death for disregard of religion "; and having shown that his hero was innocent on this count, he is insensibly drawn on to relate this and that anecdote of his conversations. On the whole, the impression left by the Socrates of Xenophon is that he represents the *ne plus ultra* of common-sense. His object is to get at the real meaning of words and things, and to give those who come to him for advice the soundest counsel possible respecting the matter in hand. For it is noticeable (and this has given offence to critics who suspect Xenophon's accuracy) that Socrates according to Xenophon does not, generally, seek out his interlocutors. He sits on a kind of Delphic tripod, and they come to him ; though sometimes he is told of a case needing counsel, and goes unasked to impart it. On the whole, the Xenophontic account of Socrates' method seems to have a

certain degree of *a priori* probability, and can be
made to harmonise with the (superficially, perhaps
contradictory) statements of Socrates himself in
the Platonic dialogues, and his practice as reported
by Diogenes Laertius. When he speaks of taking
the initiative and actually interviewing distinguished
men with the avowed object of proving that they
are really shams, belonging to the class of seeming
wise men (δοκοῦντες μὲν σοφοὶ εἶναι, ὄντες δ' οὔ), it is
obviously unnecessary to take this account *au pied
de la lettre*. One can hardly suppose that even
Socrates could have hoped to accomplish much by
thrusting himself in the path of the casual general
or politician, and subjecting him to an interpella-
tion on the first principles of his profession. More
probably the personal contact of philosopher and
examinee would be the result of some chance
meeting in the Socratic *salon*, which appears to
have been frequented by all sorts and conditions
of men,—and women too, for that matter: and
this is, in the main, what we should gather from
Xenophon. Socrates is regarded by him as the
oracle of a large circle; and as the subjects of
conversation and the doings of society are unlimited, his oracular counsels are not invariably
confined to the very highest topics. Nor, as it

must be allowed, do they fail occasionally to
remind us in their manner of the utterances of
Mr. Barlow ; but that is perhaps inevitable in the
case of a biographer like Xenophon, whose
reverence for his hero is such that it occasionally
outweighs his sense of literary fitness, and who is
not afraid to weary his readers by regarding every
social question as a riddle to which Socrates alone
has the answer. Whether the advice given was
platitudinous or not matters nothing to him,—it
was Socrates who gave it, and that is enough.
Hence it is that sometimes the philosopher discourses on the highest subjects and propounds
the highest principles of morality; while sometimes,
again, he sinks to the level of a manual of etiquette.
Constantly it is Socrates who is called in to settle
some family dispute, or to help a friend in a difficulty. There is a quarrel between two brothers,
Chaerecrates and Chaerephon (the latter one of the
inner Socratic circle, and by Aristophanes held up
to ridicule as the type and model of Socrates'
disciples): Socrates composes the feud with a short
homily on fraternal affection. One Aristarchus is
in difficulties with his female relations. Civic
troubles have deprived them of their homes, and
they have all come to live upon him, so that what

with sisters, cousins, and nieces, he has no less than
fourteen ladies consuming his substance: money is
scarce, times are hard, and poor Aristarchus does
not know what to do with them.　Socrates advises
that they should be made to work for their living:
it appears that all the women are skilled in worsted
work, so Aristarchus "bought wool"; and all the
sisters, cousins, and nieces "worked at breakfast-
time and till dinner, and became cheerful instead
of ill-tempered."　Or again, his friend Crito being
troubled by the burdens and dangers of wealth,
Socrates provides him with a protector in the shape
of one Archedemus, "eloquent and capable, but
poor"; and the arrangement is such a success that
Crito is soon freed from blackmailers and enemies
in general, and both parties regard Socrates as
their benefactor.

As has been said, Xenophon's manner of
telling these stories rather tends to recall the
inimitable prosiness of *Sandford and Merton;*
but we cannot conclude from this insignifi-
cance that they are not Socratic. Many sayings of other teachers have seemed trifling and
commonplace enough when recorded in memoirs;
yet the teacher's personal influence has been
nevertheless of the greatest.　So we may well

imagine that the remarkable personality of Socrates—the "satyr-like" exterior, the "bull-like glare" of the eyes, the extraordinarily impressive manner—would have been present to many who read Xenophon's anecdotes, and read into them much that is now inevitably lost to us.

To be practically useful was that object of Socrates' teaching on which Xenophon lays most stress. But he held that counsel, to be really useful, ought to go farther than that "cramming" which seems to have been the characteristic of some other teachers of the period. There is no royal road to success except by goodness : hence it was Socrates' object to make himself useful by teaching goodness, and by showing conclusively that it is the best policy in the long run. "It was not his intention," Xenophon says, "to make his hearers able to speak, act, or invent : he held that virtue must first be implanted in them ; for he thought that capacity in such respects, without virtue, only made men more unjust, and increased their power of wrong-doing." It is at the close of a conversation between Socrates and Aristippus the Cyrenaic that we find repeated the story of the Choice of Heracles.

" When Heracles was growing up from boyhood

to man's estate, and had come to the time when
youths show that they are now able to choose for
themselves how they will enter on life, whether by
the paths of virtue or of vice, he went away into
a solitary place and sat down, doubting which of
the paths he should take. There he saw two tall
women drawing near to him : one of them seemly
and noble to look upon, clad in white raiment,
and wearing the natural adornment of purity for
her body, modesty for her eyes, and discreetness
for her bearing ; the other made plump and soft
by nurture, adorned in such wise that her skin
was whiter and redder and her person straighter
than Nature made it, with eyes wide opened and
raiment such as should best display her charms ;
eyeing herself ever and anon, and looking to see
if any one else were admiring her, and often
glancing at her own shadow. Now when they
had come near to Heracles, the first I have named
advanced in the same fashion as before ; but the
second was fain to be beforehand with her, and
hasted to Heracles and said, 'I see, Heracles, that
thou art in doubt by which road thou wilt enter
life : take me for thy love, and I will bring thee
to the pleasantest and easiest road ; so shalt thou
taste of every delight, and live thy life through

ignorant of all things hard. For first, thou shalt
have no thought of war or business, but shalt ever
be thinking what thou canst find pleasantest to
eat or drink, what sight, sound, smell, or touch be
most delightful, what loves thou canst best enjoy,
what couches are softest for slumber; and how
thou mayest have all these things with least
trouble. And think not that thou mayest lack
that which should provide thee with these things;
there is no fear that I will bring thee to the
getting of them by toil and weariness: the labours
of others thou shalt use, nor abstain from aught
whencesoever gain may be had; for to those who
dwell with me I grant leave and licence to receive
benefit whencesoever it comes.' To this Heracles
answered: 'What is thy name, lady?' 'My
friends,' she said, 'call me Happiness, and my
enemies nickname me Vice.' With that the other
woman drew near and said, 'I too, Heracles, have
come to thee, knowing thy parents, and discerning
thy nature in their upbringing: wherefore I have
hope that if thou dost follow the path that leads
to me thou wilt verily be a good workman of
all things fair and holy, and I shall seem to thee
yet far more deserving of honour and more notable
in serving thee well; and with no promise of

pleasure will I cheat thee, but will tell thee with truth the thing that is, as the gods ordained it. Of all things truly good and fair, not one do the gods give to men without labour and carefulness. If thou wilt win the favour of the gods, thou must do the gods service. If thou wilt be loved by thy friends, to thy friends be serviceable. If thou wilt have honour from any city or the whole of Hellas, serve that city or Hellas. If it be from lands or flocks and herds that thou wilt have wealth, of thy lands and flocks and herds thou must be careful. So he that would make himself great by war, and be strong to free his friends and subdue his enemies, must learn and practise the art of war ; and he that would have a strong body must accustom his body to obey his will, and exercise it with toil and sweating.' Vice struck in and said, 'Seest thou, Heracles, how long and hard is the way to pleasure which this woman shows thee ? but I will lead thee to happiness by a short way and an easy.' 'Poor wretch,' replied Virtue, 'and what good hast thou ? or what pleasant thing canst thou know, if thou wilt do nothing for the sake of all thou dost promise ? seeing that thou waitest not even for the desire of pleasant things, but fillest thyself with all before thou desirest them, eating before hunger and drinking before thirst: thou contrivest makers of relishes that thou mayest have pleasure in eating, and gettest thee costly wines and runnest hither and thither seeking snow in summer that thou mayest have pleasure in drinking: and for thy pleasure in sleep 'tis not only thy coverlet but the framework of thy bed that thou wilt have soft; for thou art fain to sleep, not for weariness, but for lack of aught to do. And for thy loves, they are artfully engendered, natural alike and unnatural; for so dost thou teach thy friends, making them to revel by night and sleep for the most useful part of the day. Though immortal, thou hast been rejected from the company of gods, and art held in dishonour by good men: nor hast ever heard the pleasantest of all hearings,—thine own praises,—nor seen the pleasantest of all sights; for thou hast never seen any good work of thine own. Who will believe thy word, or grant thee aught at thy asking? who that is wise would brook to be of those that are thy company? who in youth have no strength of body and in age no wisdom of mind: nurtured they are through their youth in comfort and idleness, and pass through their old age in toil and squalor, ashamed

of the past, and burdened by the present, for they
have squandered all pleasures in their youth, and
hoarded only hardships for their old age. But
I dwell with gods and with good men ; no good
work human or divine is wrought without me,
and I am held in especial honour among the
gods, and among such men as are fit to honour
me. For I am a welcome helpmate to craftsmen,
a faithful guardian to householders, and kindly
comrade to their servants ; a good fellow-labourer
in peace, a strong ally in war, and the best of all
friends. Those who love me enjoy their meat and
drink with pleasure and ease ; for they forbear till
they have the desire, and sleep is pleasanter to
them than it is to the idle : they are not distressed
by foregoing it, nor for its sake are they slack in
doing their duty. Among them, the young delight
in the praises of their elders, and those who are
older are proud to be honoured by the younger ;
and while the remembrance of the deeds which
they have done is pleasant to them, they take
pleasure too in present good actions. I make them
dear to the gods, loved by their friends, honoured
by their country ; and when the fated end has come,
they lie not dishonoured and forgotten, but their
names are ever familiar and their memory green.' "

Of course it is obvious that the morality of Prodicus apologue is none of the highest. We are to be virtuous because virtue is in the long run pleasanter than vice: it is merely a balancing of one pleasure against another. The Xenophontic Socrates nowhere rises to the height of Carlyle's teaching—"Love not pleasure: love God: this is the everlasting Yea!" Still, the fable is worth repeating, partly because it represents the highest note struck in the *Memorabilia*, and partly because the spirit of it is in accordance with the simplicity and even asceticism of Socrates' own life. Xenophon says of him that he inculcated goodness less by formal teaching than by his own practice in great things alike and small—not only in the higher matters of the law, but in the everyday habits of his life. It is just this simplicity and independence of luxuries that Aristophanes scoffs at, and even the more sympathetic Alcibiades cannot understand.

We cannot leave the *Memorabilia* without especial notice of that passage in which the Xenophontic approaches in method most nearly to the Platonic Socrates—I mean the story of Euthydemus. Socrates is here employing "dialectic" as he so often uses it in the Platonic dialogues: to convince his

interlocutor of ignorance, with the ulterior design
of enabling him to start fresh and unbiassed on
the road to knowledge. Perhaps it is permissible
to say that the great dialectician appears in a
not wholly creditable light. Euthydemus' crime
apparently consists in this, that he is endeavouring
to qualify himself for public life by a study of
books, to the neglect of oral teaching. Hearing
of this implied contempt of himself and his method,
Socrates (and were we speaking of any lesser man,
we should be entitled to suspect a spirit of pique)
resolves to vindicate the greatness of " lectures,"
and the insufficiency of " independent reading."
He betakes himself with a throng of friends to a
saddler's shop which Euthydemus, too young to
frequent the *agora* itself, makes his " house of call."
Here he proceeds to " draw " Euthydemus by
talking *at* him of the folly of supposing that
public life requires no preliminary training. The
object of his remarks is very much on his guard
against being entrapped into discussion, feeling
himself probably no match for so dangerous a
catechiser as Socrates. At the next interview,
" seeing that Euthydemus was on the point of
quitting the circle, and careful to avoid the appearance of admiring Socrates for his wisdom,"

Socrates proceeds to banter him with solemn gibes.

"'From Euthydemus' practice,' said he, 'it is quite clear what he will do when he is grown up. He will never shrink from taking part in any public debate. And I think indeed that his care to avoid the semblance of learning anything from any one provides him with an admirable preface to his speeches : he will begin somewhat like this :—Men of Athens ! no one has ever taught me anything : nor have I ever courted the friendship of those whom I heard of as being capable in speech and act : nor have I been the pupil of any man of knowledge. Quite the contrary : I have always been unwilling not only to be but to be thought to be any one's pupil ; but still I propose to offer you such advice as my unaided intelligence suggests. Would not this be an excellent preface for a man who wished the State to give him, for instance, the post of public physician ?' Everybody laughed at this opening "—and poor Euthydemus, one may suppose, felt rather out of countenance, and saw that he was in the toils already. After a few more interviews of the same kind, he is apparently more and more inclined to listen : and Socrates considers that the way has now been prepared for a *tête-à-tête* conversation. Seeking out Euthydemus alone, he convicts the unfortunate youth (it must be admitted, by the most unblushingly sophistical arguments, such as the Platonic Socrates holds up to derision), that he really knows nothing of what an intending statesman ought to know : it is shown that what is conventionally termed just may also be proved unjust, and that what is generally esteemed as good may quite possibly be bad. Euthydemus can define nothing satisfactorily,—that is, in such a way that Socrates cannot stultify the definition ; and eventually " he went away very much dispirited, despising himself, and convinced that he was in very truth a slave. Many of those who were similarly treated by Socrates gave up associating with him, and he thought the worse of them for it " ; but Euthydemus' humble desire to learn was stronger than his self-conceit, and he became one of Socrates' most devoted disciples. So the State lost a servant and Socrates gained a pupil.

Whether or not this conversation ever really took place must be a matter of doubt : at any rate neither Xenophon nor any of his friends heard it ; but it has sufficient *a priori* probability. The dialectic method is that which is more skilfully

managed by Plato : the arguments are tinged with
that sophistry which Aristophanes ridicules in the
Clouds—that " too clever by half" cleverness which
sees every side of a question, and therefore encour-
ages hesitation rather than action. Doubtless the
Socratic method was not good for every one : the
best servants of the State are often those who can
only see from one point of view.

M

CHAPTER IX

THE 'CLOUDS'

EVERY small town—small enough for the personal peculiarities of its inhabitants to be familiar—is in itself the potential birthplace of an Aristophanic comedy; nothing being more universally and eternally interesting than personal gossip and scandal.

> " There lies the village below us, and looks so quiet and still,
> And yet bubbles o'er like a city with gossip and scandal
> and spite."

That is really an optimistic view of village life; Tennyson's village, if it was like other small English communities, was not only as scandalous as any city, but far more so. But at Athens it was not only the small size and the exclusive self-centred interests of a Greek πόλις which particularly favoured the development of the old comedy: there was this difference between modern—at least English—and Athenian life, that whereas with us a man's life is less open to the search-light of public opinion, because even journalism cannot always penetrate the domestic castle, an Athenian citizen lived, moved, and had his being in the street, the *agora*, the Pnyx—in short, his domestic or indoor life was altogether secondary and unimportant; he was not primarily a householder and ratepayer, but a *boulevardier* going to and fro in the full light of day, and exposed at every turn to the pitiless shafts of the street satirist. Matter thus provided by this universal publicity, the very spirit of Athens was a curiosity "always wishing to hear or tell some new thing"; and a keen, uncharitable, straightforward criticism unhampered by glosses and euphemisms, reproducing observed objects with the unfeeling candour of a phonograph or an amateur photographer. Thus it appears that to Aristophanes—at least in his earlier comedies—absolutely nothing is sacred, and the personal peculiarities of the man in the street are just as fair game as Alcibiades' lisp or Euripides' mother.

To us it may sometimes seem rather surprising that Aristophanes, with a genius which certainly could have been independent of local personalities, should have chosen to confine it within the limits of a small town, and to fill his plays with libellous attacks which are often wholly gratuitous, and not connected in any way with the plot—mere side-shots in passing : the rule of ὀνομαστὶ μὴ κωμῳδεῖν, "no personalities on the stage"—a law which Aristophanes himself lived to see in operation—has penetrated and prejudiced us so deeply that the best public opinion regards public allusion to individual foibles as indecent and almost criminal. But Athenian comedy—that is, the older comedy—was hampered by no such prejudices, and the reason of course why Aristophanes chose so to restrict his field of observation was that the material for the satirist, given liberty of speech, was immense within the walls of Athens ; and, moreover, he was as little troubled as most Greeks about the relative unimportance of the actual world he lived in. To him Hellas was the centre of the universe, and Athens was the centre of Hellas ; just as Thucydides professes to believe that the petty and futile struggle known as the Peloponnesian War was the most important series of events in all history. For posterity, after all, the delusion was a fortunate one.

Except in the matter of literary taste—for it is hard to believe that the *average* Athenian could share Aristophanes' preference of Aeschylus to Euripides—Aristophanes consistently represents

the view of the *homme moyen sensuel.* He plays
to the bourgeois gallery, which is essentially conservative, an advocate of the established order.
It seems to be a common tradition that the great
comedian was bribed by Anytus and Meletus,
Socrates' enemies and subsequent persecutors, to
attack him on the stage: the comedy of the
Clouds was to be a sort of *ballon d'essai* to
test public opinion : be this true or not, the
genesis of the play (produced about twenty years
before Socrates' death) is natural and reasonable
enough. To Aristophanes Socrates was an-
tagonistic, as a representative of those pestilent
questionings of the established ideas of right and
wrong which tended to make the younger generation dissatisfied with the simple ideals of its
fathers ; while in his assumption of the character
of the good easy man who takes the enjoyments
of life as he finds them, he found it in his *rôle* to
regard the Socratic asceticism as a mere eccen-
tricity not only foolish in itself but implying a
reflection on the "lax habit" of the average
Athenian. To the ordinary man the Socratic
circle would be nothing but "poor devils"—ὁ
κακοδαίμων Σωκράτης καὶ Χαιρεφῶν.

The contrast of youth and age, old ideas and

new, is the stock-in-trade of comedy. But it is
only since Menander that the *jeune premier* has the
last word : in Aristophanes, youth is generally
foolish, and foolish for want of the rod, which was
more freely administered in the brave days of old.
In the *Clouds* the particular aspect of young Athens
is its crude receptivity. Strepsiades, the "heavy
father" of the piece, is indeed just as crude as his
son, but is endowed with the saving virtue of
stupidity, and atones for his temporary aberration
by coming to a full sense of his misdeeds at the
end of the play. This Strepsiades is an excellent
type of the rustic as we know him in all ages : old-
fashioned in his instincts and beliefs, without any
safeguard of principle—religious without morality—
so that once his pocket is appealed to he is acces-
sible to any new ideas ; of which, however, he can
only grasp a very superficial part. His son Pheidippides is an Athenian *gommeux* who squanders his
father's money on the turf. Strepsiades has heard
that there are some clever people at Athens who
can teach you how not to pay your debts—

"*Strepsiades.* Go, I entreat you, dearest son of
    mine,
Go and be taught. *Pheidippides.* And what, pray,
    shall I learn ?

Str. I'm told they have two Reasons—one the
　　better
(Whatever that may mean), and one the worse ;
The worse of these two Reasons, so they say,
Puts forward unjust pleas, and always wins.
Now, if you were to learn this unjust reasoning,
Of all the debts that I've incurred for you
I would not pay one creditor a penny."

However, Pheidippides will not go and learn—
so Strepsiades has to go himself.

The " Phrontisterion," or Thinking-shop, is probably a creation of Aristophanes' own. We know
nothing of a "school" of Socratics localised in
any definite habitation. On Strepsiades' arrival
Socrates and his disciples are represented as sitting
together, and proposing to each other frivolous
questions of "science falsely so called "—

" ('Twas asked by Socrates of Chaerephon
How many of its own feet a flea could jump ;
For one bit Chaerephon upon the eyebrow
And hopped from thence on to the Master's head),"

that is to say, the disciples lie grovelling on their
faces, while Socrates himself swings suspended in
a basket or on a perch—"I walk on air and con-
template the sun," he explains to Strepsiades.

The old rustic proposes to become a pupil, and
is ready to swear "by the gods" that he will pay
whatever sum Socrates asks—an oath taken in a
temple being the usual form of promise to pay
between tutor and pupil, as we learn from the
Protagoras;—and this reference to the gods serves
to introduce the Chorus of Clouds, the deities who
are supposed to inspire the nebulous speculations
of Socrates and other sophists.

> "*Soc.* Would you then know about the spheres
>   divine,
> Their nature true? *Str.* Yes—if they but exist.
>   *Soc.* And would you fain hold converse with the
>   Clouds,
> Our deities? *Str.* Most certainly I would.
>   *Soc.* Be seated then upon the sacred stool.
>   *Str.* There, I am seated. *Soc.* Then put on this
>   crown.
>   *Str.* A crown? What for the crown? Ah,
>   Socrates,
> Don't sacrifice me, like poor Athamas!

>   *   *   *   *   *

>   *Soc.* Thy peace thou must hold, O questioner old,
>   till our solemn entreaty be ended.
> Hear thou my prayer, thou measureless Air, the
>   Earth who sustainest suspended!

Thou Ether so bright, and ye Clouds in the height,
    dread bearers of lightning and thunder,
Great goddesses, hear, and arise and appear, for
    the Thinker to worship and wonder!
    Str. Not yet, not yet—I'm afraid of the wet—let
    me first put a mantle or wrap on :
To think from my home that I ventured to come,
    without even so much as a cap on!
    Soc. O come, I implore, ye Clouds we adore, that
    the learner may see and may know ye!
Whether still on the crest of Olympus ye rest, 'mid
    his pinnacles sacred and snowy,
Be ye weaving the dance in their far-away haunts
    with the bands of Oceanus' daughters,
Be ye waiting awhile, by the fountains of Nile, to
    replenish your urns with his waters,
Be ye gathering low upon Mimas his snow, or
    descending on marshes Maeotian,
O deign to delight in our mystical rite, and appear
    for our words of devotion !

    Then the song of the Clouds is heard in the
distance.

    Rise to the view, daughters of dew,
    Clouds that eternally float in the blue!
    Higher, O, higher

Rise from the surges of Ocean our sire;
Up to the forest-clad mountains, where we,
Gazing, may see
Far on the plain, garden and grain
Fed by the holy beneficent earth,
Rushing of river and roaring of firth:
Ever unwearied on high
Flashes the firmament's eye:
Sisters, again
Doff we our mantle of vapour and rain,
Gaze in our godhead on mountain and plain."

Then the Clouds are descried coming over the heights of Parnes—visible, of course, from an open-air stage; and when they come near they are represented in the theatre by a Chorus of Women —whom Strepsiades finds it hard to identify with the Clouds of his experience, "for these," he says, "have noses." Socrates explains to him why they have taken a female form, and goes on to assure him that

"It is these whom alone we as deities own: all
    else is mere fables and lying.
  Str. Great Earth! that is odd—and is Zeus
    not a god? sure his deity's past the denying.
  Soc. Nay, from prating desist—your Zeus doesn't
    exist!

Str. No Zeus? I can hardly believe it:
Then perhaps you'll explain what occasions the
    rain, if it isn't from him we receive it.
Soc. Why, my answer is pat—'tis the Clouds
    who give that, for it comes when they loom
    and they gather:
Were it sent us by Zeus, they'd be no sort of
    use: he would rain in the clearest of weather."

Eventually Strepsiades, after passing a short
"entrance examination," is admitted to the school,
and disappears half pleased and half frightened
into the Thinking-shop. However, it turns out
that Socrates cannot do anything with him. He
forgets what he learns, and gives absurd answers to
the Master's questions ; and at last Socrates gives
it up in despair.

"*Soc.* Go to the deuce! begone! I'll none of you,
Stupid, forgetful, miserable dotard!
Str. Alas, poor me! and what's to happen now?
'Twill be my ruin not to learn to quibble.
O Clouds, I pray you, give me some advice!
Chorus. Our counsel, aged sir, is simply this:
If you've a son who's come to man's estate,
Just send him here to learn instead of you.
Str. Yes, I've a son, a real gentleman:

But he won't learn : so what am I to do ?

 Chorus. What ! and you humour him ?

      Str. He's stout and lusty—
His mother's family are folk of fashion—
Still, I'll go fetch him—and if he won't come
Most certainly I'll turn him out of doors.
Go in, please, Socrates ; I'll be back directly."

  *   *   *   *   *

Modern criticism is perhaps rather too apt to
dwell exclusively on the aesthetic side of Greek
character, so much so as to obscure the fact that
a moral ideal, and the difficulty of attaining it, is
a common theme with Greek writers. Yet the
"parting of the ways," the difficulty and beauty
of Virtue as contrasted with the ease and ugliness
of Vice, is one of the commonplaces of Hellenic
literature : witness—to say nothing of the teaching
of the Platonic and Xenophontic Socrates—its
legends of the Judgment of Paris and the Choice
of Heracles ; or such well-known passages as
Hesiod's comparison of Vice and Virtue—

"Vice is a gift that all may lightly win :
Near doth she dwell, and smooth the road of sin :
But Virtue nought save labour may ensue,
And steep and long the path that leads thereto,

Yea, rough at first: but once the heights are
gained,
Lightly the meed is kept, though hardly 'twas
attained."

The dispute between the Just and Unjust Reason,
as to which shall have the privilege of instructing
Pheidippides, runs on the same lines as the contention between Vice and Virtue in Prodicus' apologue :
Just Reason is identified with that old-fashioned
austerity and obedience to rule which made the
heroes of Marathon and Salamis, and laid the
foundations of Athenian greatness; Unjust Reason
is the personified principle of "Fay ce que voudras,"
that dangerous moral latitude which Aristophanes
held to be the necessary outcome of a shelving of
ancient social tradition, and an increased though
natural attention to personal comforts. The Δίκαιος
Λόγος enlarges eloquently on the beauty of the old
Athenian *régime*—

" Now first you must know, in the days long ago,
    how we brought up our youngsters and
    schooled them ;
When to argument just 'twas the fashion to
    trust, and when Virtue and Modesty ruled
    them.

Little boys—'twas averred—must be seen and not
    heard; and to school they must go all together;
Unprotected by coats, or by wraps for their throats,
    in the coldest and snowiest weather.
Where they learnt to repeat, in a posture discreet,
    all the ancient respectable ditties,
Such as 'Sound of the war that is borne from
    afar,' or 'Pallas, the sacker of cities;'
And to render with care the traditional air,
    without any newfangled vagary:
If you played the buffoon, or the simple old
    tune if you tried to embellish or vary,
And to show off your skill in a shake or a trill, or
    in modern fantastical ruses,—
All you got by your trick was a touch of the
    stick, for the outrage you did to the Muses."

Submit yourself to be trained in these lines
(says the Just Reason) and you will live a virtuous
life, doing nothing base, "because you are going
to remodel the Statue of Honour." Whatever the
world may say about you, "at any rate you shall
pass your time in the gymnasia, fresh and in good
condition"—

"And you never will pose as a maker of *mots*, or
    of phrases of modern invention,

And you'll wholly withdraw from the snares of
    the law, and its petty and knavish contention;
With a garland bedight of the reedflower white,
    to the Academe's olive trees shady
You shall daily resort for your leisure or sport,
    with a playfellow sober and steady;
While the pine and the plane sing a whispered
    refrain, and the spring shall delectably scent
    ye
With an odorous breeze from the flowers and
    the trees, and a savour of *dolce far niente.*"

However, the Unjust Reason has no difficulty in
showing that these methods and ideals are quite
obsolete and absurd, and eventually wins the day,
and carries off Pheidippides; who presently re-
appears instructed in all the wisdom of the sophists,
so that his father is now fully armed with arguments
to baffle the attacks of his creditors. This is all
very well; but Strepsiades presently finds that he
has made a Frankenstein monster who is too
strong for him. The newfangled ideas of the
Socratic school will not mix with the old traditions
of an elder generation : a quarrel at dinner leads
to a painful domestic scene, and Strepsiades is
beaten by his son.

"So first I bade him play and sing" [says the
unfortunate father, relating his woes to the
Chorus] "some such familiar piece as

The 'Ram' of old Simonides, and how they
shore his fleeces.

He answered straight, You're out of date—the
times you're quite behind, sir!

At meals to sing is not the thing, except for
maids who grind, sir.'"

(*Pheidippides interrupts.*) "Ay, that itself deserved
the stick: what person ever made a

Suggestion that his guests should sing and chirp
like a cicada?"

"Yes (*continues Strepsiades*) that's precisely
what he said, exactly as you hear it,

And told me that Simonides was destitute of merit.

I stood it well enough at first, although 'twas
hard forbearing:

'Well, sing,' I said, 'some Aeschylus; p'r'aps
he'll be worth the hearing.'

'What, Aeschylus?' the youth replied; 'not,
father, if I know it—

You surely don't suppose that I call Aeschylus
a poet?

A mere bombastic blusterer, replete with sound
and fury!'

To hear him talk quite sickened me—it did, I
   do assure ye ;
But still I answered peaceably, controlling of
   my passion,
' Let's have, then, something written in your precious
   modern fashion.'
Whereon he reeled a *morceau* off quite up to
   date and recent,
A story from Euripides, which really wasn't
   decent !
'Twas horrid, and I told him so—my wrath I
   could not smother—
And each reproach I hurled at him he answered
   with another ;
Till, as we wrangled up and down, he suddenly
   attacks me,
And kicks and nearly throttles me, and pummels
   me and whacks me ! "

Pheidippides, however, is not in the least ashamed
of himself. He is proud of his emancipation from
old-fashioned traditions, and actually proposes to
convince Strepsiades—quite in the best manner of
Euripides—that a son has a perfect right to beat
his father if he pleases : nay, that it may even be
a duty.

N

"'When I was young did you to me administer
    correction?'

'Of course I did—it showed my care and natural
    affection.'

'Well, 'tis in just the self-same way that I by you
    am dealing—

I beat you just to show my love and proper filial
    feeling!

I'm sure it can't be just or right your floggings
    should be fewer

Than those that I received from you: I'm quite as
    free as you were.

Then, if you say to beat a child is merely human
    nature—

An aged man's a child again, of rather larger
    stature:

And all the more he needs the rod, for, when you
    catch him tripping,

He has not the excuse of youth to save him from
    a whipping.'

'But everywhere 'tis held a crime—by no tradition
    backed 'tis!'

'Well, 'twas a man in days of old who penalised
    the practice,

Just a mere man like you or me, his fellows who
    persuaded,

And if I make another law, I simply do what they
   did :
If they passed bills for beating sons, then surely I
   should gather
That I've a right to pass a bill for sons to beat
   their father:
Though, 'spite the stripes we sons received ere this
   my legislation,
We don't propose to claim arrears, nor ask for
   compensation.'"

Then Pheidippides goes on to show that by the
same arguments he is entitled to beat his mother
too ; which Strepsiades cannot stand, although he
could apparently have made up his mind to take a
beating himself. Now, however, when he sees
himself the victim of difficulties of his own making,
he remonstrates with the Clouds for having encouraged him to go to school with Socrates : the
Chorus reply that Strepsiades' infatuation was really
a special providence to convince him of the folly
of new ideas, and with the consolatory assurance
that all his misfortunes are meant for his good,
he is left to get out of trouble as best he can—
which he does by setting fire to the Phrontisterion.
So the play closes with the destruction of the

den of sophists, and the triumph of Athenian conservatism.

Unless Aristophanes was particularly ill-informed, or Plato, Xenophon, and the tradition of the world are all at fault, the great comedian must have recognised the cruel injustice of associating Socrates with the influence of the Unjust Reason. So far as we know, to accuse such a teacher of inculcating moral laxity or encouraging youth in ultra-democratic licence would be the very height of absurdity. But Aristophanes, as we have seen, was convinced that the world of his own childhood was the best of all possible worlds ; that justice lay on the side of the wisdom of our fathers, and injustice on the side of any ideas, moral or immoral, that tended to " unsettle." He was the very apostle of the *status quo ;* and as such, waging war against the great army of innovators, he made Socrates by implication responsible for the ἄδικος λόγος simply because it happened that Socrates was prominent among those who, for various reasons, were dissatisfied with the *status quo* at Athens. Nor can it be denied that Aristophanes' position had a certain basis of reasonableness. He saw the danger of removing the sanction of tradition from before the eyes of a people only too quick to assimilate all ideas, bad and good alike; and certainly, if political decadence can be associated with social laxity, the bitterness of his satire on the Athenian youth *fin de siècle* was justified by later experience.

CHAPTER X

IN 399 B.C., being then seventy years old, Socrates was summoned before the Athenian dicastery, to answer the charges of corrupting the young by his teaching, and professing his disbelief in the national gods. His accusers were three: Meletus, Anytus, and Lycon.

Socrates' so-called *Apologia* on this occasion is really anything but a serious defence against the charges adduced. They were indeed, under the circumstances, practically unanswerable: vaguely-worded accusations of infidelity and the promulgation of demoralising doctrines were not matters to be discussed before a jury composed of some five hundred casually-chosen Athenian citizens. Moreover, Socrates had been before the Athenian public as a teacher for at least thirty years. To all who cared to acquaint themselves with it, his teaching and the inferences to be drawn from it

were already sufficiently familiar. His antecedents
should have been his best defence. To men of
intelligence, any formal rebutting of his accusers'
charges was unnecessary : to appeal to the unin-
telligent was impossible. Thus the speech—
whether actually delivered in substance or put
into his mouth by Plato—is but little concerned
with answering the formal indictment. Treating
this as insincere and unworthy of any serious
consideration, Socrates dismisses it in a few per-
functory paragraphs with a contemptuous brevity :
that part of the *Apology* which has really an
enduring interest for us is the philosopher's review
of the real reasons which have rendered him unpopular, and that " profession of faith " in defiance
of all verdicts which entitles the *Apology* to the
place it has always occupied in literature. But it
is no plea for acquittal. Socrates knows the mind
of his countrymen too well to expect any other
than an adverse verdict—indeed he hardly desires
not to be condemned.

" What is against me in this case," he says
in effect, " is not idle and unreasonable assertions
such as those contained in the indictment :
it is rather the state of public opinion and
popular prejudice. For one thing, the public

mind is possessed by the idea of a certain sceptic, always inquiring about matters in heaven and under the earth with which he has no concern, and making the worse appear the better reason. That is the Socrates of Aristophanes. But every one who knows me is well aware that this caricature of me has no likeness to reality. I have never ventured on any physical speculations.

"Then there is another reason for my unpopularity. Some time ago the Delphic oracle declared me to be the wisest man on earth. As I could not understand how this could be, I was moved to question certain persons who had the reputation for wisdom, to see if they were really less wise than they appeared. I found that they were so ; and having discovered their real ignorance I tried to convince them of the fact,—which did not make me popular with persons of established reputation. And ever since it has been my practice to go about exposing shams, and making enemies in consequence.

"And moreover," he continues, "young men of leisure, sons of wealthy fathers, follow me about ; and it is not my fault if they take pleasure in listening to my examinations. They often imitate me, and then go on to examine others ; when, I am sure, they find that there is no lack of instances of this semblance without the reality of knowledge. As a result of this, their victims are angry with *me*, not with themselves; they begin to talk about the pestilent doctrines of Socrates and his corrupting influence on the young. Ask them to point to any act or doctrine of mine with this tendency, and they have nothing to say, because they know of none; but rather than seem at a loss for an answer they will repeat the vulgar charges against all seekers of knowledge, and tell you that I discourse about the upper air and the centre of the earth, and teach youths to disbelieve in the gods, and to make the worse appear the better reason. Of course they do not like to confess, what is the truth, that their pretence of knowledge without reality is being exposed. There are numbers of these persons, all keen and vehement, and their assertions are plausible and systematically made; so that they have long been dinning these acrimonious calumnies into your ears. Such are my assailants, Meletus, Anytus, and Lycon,—Meletus, who is concerned to avenge the poets; Anytus, the professional craftsmen and politicians; and Lycon, the rhetoricians. So that I repeat what I began by saying—it would be surprising if I were able to rid your minds in a moment of their long-standing misconceptions." Then, after a very short answer to the specific charges as to infidelity and corruption of youth, Socrates sums up the matter by saying, " What I shall be worsted by—if indeed I am—is not Meletus nor Anytus, but the calumnies and jealousies of the many.

" Well, but it may be urged that if I make enemies by this course I ought to discontinue it. Why run the risk of death? To this I answer that I do not fear death; did I fear it, I should be guilty of that baseless assumption of knowledge which I blame in others. This search after truth is a task imposed on me by God, a task which I will perform in scorn of consequence. 'Here stand I: I can no other.' Acquit me or not as you will: know only that I will do nothing else than what I do now, if I am to die many deaths for it." Such is the gist of the argument.

Socrates having concluded his address, the votes of the jury were taken, and a small majority pronounced him guilty of the charges named in the indictment. This, however, did not involve the ratification of the penalty—death—proposed by the prosecution; according to the Athenian law the other side might propose an amendment, and

the jury would then decide which penalty was to
be inflicted.   Socrates then, acting as he says
under protest and at the instance of his friends,
assessed his crime at a fine of thirty minae, which
sum Plato and some others undertook to pay.
But if the court were to requite him according to
his real deserts, they should (he said) not only not
punish him at all, but rather award him, as a benefactor to society, the greatest honour which the
State of Athens could bestow on any of its members
—the perpetual right of dining in the Prytaneium,
or public hall.

Again the votes were taken, and again a majority
sided with Socrates' accusers : he was condemned
to death.   His fate thus decided, he once more
rose to speak, addressing himself in turn to the
two sections of the jury, who had voted for acquittal and condemnation respectively.   To the latter
he prophesied, with the weighty utterance of a man
doomed to death, that the blood of the first martyr
would be the seed of philosophic inquiry.   Let them
not suppose that by killing Socrates they had rid
themselves of unpopular teachers ; rather these
would increase in numbers.   For those who had
voted for his acquittal (and no doubt some of
these must have been moved by actual friendship

as much as by a sense of justice) he strikes the
note that resounds through the pages of the
Phaedo. Death can in no case be an actual evil.
Either it is a simple negation of everything, or it is
—at least to the just man—a positive good. " And
now," he concludes, " it is time that we should
depart — I to death, you to life. But which of
us goes to the better thing, only God knows."

Grote, holding a brief for the Athenian Demos,
finds the condemnation of Socrates less unintelli-
gible, after reading the speech for the defence. It
is at least reasonable not to make the sublimity
of that defence an additional count against the
dicasts who recorded their votes for Meletus ; for
—except in so far as the jury might be won by the
piquant novelty of a defendant who deliberately
refused to employ the customary appeals *ad miseri-
cordiam*—no court composed for the most part of
ordinary unphilosophic men would be likely to
find in the *Apology* any particular reasons for
acquitting one whose real crime in their eyes was
no specific doctrine, no particular instance of irre-
ligious conduct, but a general reputation for
" advanced opinions." None the less, the condemnation of Socrates remains one of the most
surprising facts in history. Grant the temper that

could listen seriously to the indictment and the rest follows : but what surprises is the temper.

Living after all the ages of persecution and intolerance and martyrdom for conscience' sake, we are perhaps inclined to dwell too little on Socrates' execution, and to regard it as the natural consummation which it might have been under the tyranny of a Nero or an Inquisition. But none the less it remains one of the surprises of history—a surprise even to Athens herself, once the deed was done. The Athenians were not religious fanatics. They allowed Aristophanes to burlesque their gods. Obviously, Socrates was not put to death from any sincere conviction in the minds of thinking men that he was really a bolder innovator or really a worse " corrupter of youth " than any of the contemporary reformers of Greek thought. Not to mention the popular poet Euripides, who can venture to say in the face of Athens, " 'Tis law that bids us believe in the gods,"—even Sophocles, even Aeschylus himself, is far removed from a literal acceptance of the current mythology. Apart from the caricature of Aristophanes, nothing would lead us to suppose that Socrates did not accept as much of the contemporary religion of Hellas as any other

intelligent Athenian. Xenophon lays stress upon
the fact that his master was especially careful of
ceremonial observance. Nor is it intelligible why
—granting the danger of his principles and practice—his accusation should have been delayed till
he was seventy years old, and could not remain much
longer to trouble the minds of respectable citizens.

Yet no doubt the ignorant mass of the voters
who passed sentence of death was really influenced
by the terms of the indictment (stating as it did
that Socrates introduced a new religion and thereby corrupted the minds of young men), and really
persuaded that Socrates was a dangerous innovator.
Most men are slow to realise change, and all the
more shocked by it when the realisation comes;
and the particular aspect of change which is first
brought home to their consciousness is naturally
identified with the whole process. The majority
of the dicasts being presumably possessed of no
greater degree of intelligence than any large body
of men, were probably unconscious of the rapid
growth of new ideas around them; they had not
fully realised that their old religion was melting
away before influences much stronger than that of
any individual teacher: and the statement that
Socrates taught the worship of new gods came

upon them as an illuminating surprise which convinced them for the moment that it was he and no other who was responsible for that change which was now first presented to them in a concrete form. They would naturally forget that, after all, the whole teaching of their favourite dramatists had really done much more than Socrates to " corrupt youth."

Moreover, a further reason may be found in the circumstances of the time. Athens had been deeply humiliated, first by the lamentable end of her great Sicilian expedition, and finally by the closing disasters of the Peloponnesian War, and was probably ready to make any one the scapegoat of her misfortunes. What befell Socrates might just as well have happened at this particular moment to any other teacher ; only it happened that it was against him that Anytus and Meletus had a private grudge ; and so Socrates, 'the all-wise, the harmless nightingale of the Muses,' was made the Jonah of the ship of State, because the generation which he taught had been less brave and less fortunate than their grandfathers who had fought at Marathon.

It was chronicled in Athenian legend that Minos,

sovereign of Crete, had avenged upon Athens the
death of his son Androgeos by exacting from her
an annual tribute of seven youths and seven
maidens, as a sacrifice to the Cretan monster
called the Minotaur. Now when this human
tribute was the third time despatched from
Attica, it chanced that one of the seven youths
was the hero Theseus ; who slew the monster and
thereby relieved his countrymen for ever from the
odious necessity imposed upon them. In this
exploit he had been favoured by Apollo, and to
the Delian god Theseus had vowed a vow that, in
the event of his success, the ship in which he and
his fellow-victims were sailing to Crete should every
year be sent to take part in the great Apolline
festival at Delos. Ever since then—so ran the
legend—the vow had been faithfully performed.
Every year a sacred vessel sailed to Delos for the
festival ; and in the time that elapsed between her
departure and her return to the Piraeus, the city of
Athens must be kept free from all pollution, and
no man might be put to death within its walls.
So it happened that in 399 B.C. the ship had sailed
a day before Socrates' trial and condemnation, and
therefore the execution of the condemned man
must of necessity be postponed till the vessel

returned from her mission. Socrates thus remained in prison for a month. During this period
he was apparently not treated with particular
severity. Athenian gaol regulations were not
inconveniently strict ; the prison was opened every
day (so says the narrator of the *Phaedo*), when
Socrates was allowed to see a large number of
friends ; and it appears that had he chosen he
might have escaped without difficulty. His friend
Crito, in the dialogue called by that name, urges
him at the eleventh hour to avail himself of the
opportunity and withdraw to Thessaly. Possibly
the authorities were ready enough to connive, and
so to save Athens from the odium of his execution.
Socrates, however, declined, as he said, to " disobey
the laws " ; and it was perhaps natural enough that
he should hardly have cared to gain a decade or so
of life at the expense of his consistency and his
reputation.

The dialogue entitled *Phaedo* has for its argument the immortality of the soul ; and for its
setting, the closing scene of the great teacher's
life. It is his last day on earth ; the sacred ship
has returned to the Piraeus. Socrates has been
loosed from his fetters, and is sitting at ease among

o

the friends who have come to pay him their last visit. These may be held to have constituted the "inner circle" of Socrates' disciples. Fifteen are named—Athenians and aliens; none of them otherwise well known to history, or even elsewhere mentioned—except Crito—as Socrates' personal friends. It is especially stated that Plato was ill, and therefore absent; and Chaerephon, Socrates' most faithful associate, was dead.

"I will try to tell you" (the speaker is Phaedo himself) "the whole story. I and the rest had made it our custom to spend the preceding days with Socrates, meeting at dawn in the court where the trial was held; it was close to the prison. So we used always to wait about and talk to each other till the prison doors were opened, which was not early; and as soon as ever they were thrown open we used to go in to Socrates' cell and generally spent the day with him. On the present occasion we had met earlier than usual, for on coming out of the prison the preceding evening we learnt that the ship had arrived from Delos; we therefore arranged to meet at the accustomed spot as early as possible. When we had come, the porter, who usually answered us, came out and bade us wait, and not come in till he should give

us word : ' the Eleven,' he said, ' are loosing Socrates,
and telling him how he is to-day to be put to
death.' Well, after a short time he came back and
bade us come in. We did so, and found Socrates
freed from his fetters, and Xanthippe—you know
her—sitting by him with his boy. She, when she
saw us, cried out dolefully, ' Alas, Socrates! this
is the last time you and your friends will converse
together !' or used some such womanlike expression. Socrates turned to Crito and said, ' Ask
some one to take her away home '; so she was
taken off by some of Crito's servants, wailing and
lamenting. Socrates then sat up on his couch,
and bent his leg and rubbed it, saying as he did
so, ' What a strange thing, friends, is this so-called
pleasure ! how curiously it is related to pain, which
seems its contrary ! you can never have the two
together, yet if you seek and find the one you are
almost compelled to take the other too.' " Thus,
he says, the pain caused by the fetter necessarily
brings pleasure when he is released.

The dialogue on the immortality of the soul,
which follows this introduction, is a conversation
in which none take part but the intimate friends
and pupils of Socrates ; thus it is characterised
throughout—although the subject is in the highest

degree controversial, and the doctrine one that
even Socrates' immediate circle is hardly strong
enough to grasp—by a complete absence of all
such hostility and bitterness on the part of the
disputants as we find in the *Gorgias*, for instance.
The philosopher needs none of the weapons which
he has been accustomed to use against opponents
who are prejudiced against him from the outset.
This, more than any other of Plato's dialogues, is
calmly and soberly reasoned from beginning to
end. The two young Thebans, Cebes and Simmias,
state the doubts natural to the popular mind and
their own with candour and temperance ; and
Socrates answers them in a similar spirit. So the
argument holds the even tenor of its way, "Ohne
Hast aber auch ohne Rast," through all difficulties
to the conclusion.

Socrates had said to the dicasts in court, " You
go hence to life, and I to death ; but which of
these is the better, God knows." Now he advances
a step further. Death is better than life, because
it is the separation of soul and body ; and only
when it is freed from the body can the soul attain
to true knowledge. But how, it is naturally asked,
can we be sure that the soul has any life apart
from the body ? To this there is a double answer.

It is a law of nature that opposites should alternate. Waking follows sleep, death follows life; and it is a natural conclusion that life again should be born of death—life, whether here again on earth or elsewhere. Moreover, the doctrine of ἀνάμνησις here and elsewhere proved—the doctrine that all learning is a reminding, a reminiscence of what was previously known—points clearly to the truth that the soul must have lived somewhere before its mortal birth—

> " Not in entire forgetfulness,
> And not in utter nakedness,
> But trailing clouds of glory, do we come
> From God, who is our home."

These two arguments together prove the life of the soul apart from the body : the second its pre-existence ; the first its existence after death.

Yet popular instinct is often stronger than reasoned truth. We have to face the vulgar fear that the poor weak soul may be actually blown away and scattered to the four winds of heaven in its passage from the mortal tenement. " This is a cauld and eerie night," said the Scotch lady on her deathbed, according to Dean Ramsay, " for me to be fleeing through the air !" But the soul (Socrates answers) is strong, and more durable than the body; the stronger, the less it has partaken in life of the bodily nature ; the more completely

Mortalem exemit labens purumque reliquit
Aetherium sensum atque aurai simplicis ignem,

so much the more likely is it to enter into eternal life with the gods.

But even so, the question is not fully answered.

"Now when Socrates had thus spoken, there was silence for a long time, and Socrates himself was to all appearance absorbed in the foregoing discussion, as were most of us. But Cebes and Simmias talked a little to each other, and Socrates, noticing them, asked what it was. 'Are you dissatisfied with what has been said ?   Indeed, if one is to discuss it thoroughly, one will find still plenty of room for suspicion and objection.   If it is anything else that you are considering, I say nothing ; but if this is your difficulty, do not hesitate yourselves to point out any better way of argument that occurs to you, and to invoke my assistance if you think that that will make matters easier.' Then Simmias said : ' Well, Socrates, I will tell you the truth.   Both of us have long felt a difficulty, and we have each been trying to make the other speak ; we wish to hear you, but are unwilling to be vexatious and tiresome to you in your hour of trouble.' Socrates replied, with a quiet smile, 'Nonsense, Simmias! truly it must be a hard matter to persuade the rest of men that I do not consider my present fate a trouble, when I cannot persuade even you of it, and you fear that I am more peevish than I have hitherto been. It seems that you think I am a worse prophet than the swans. They, when they perceive that they must die, sing more than ever they did in their lives, because they are glad to be on the point of departing into the presence of that god whose servants they are. Men, however, are moved by their own fear of death to malign the swans, and to imagine that they sing a dirge for their death and a song of sorrow,—forgetting that no bird sings when it is suffering any pain, such as hunger or cold, no, not even the swallow and nightingale and hoopoe, which are supposed to sing dirges in sorrow. But it is not, as I think, for sorrow that the swans sing, any more than any other bird; it is because they belong to Apollo, and have the gift of prophecy, and foresee the happiness of the other world; therefore it is that they sing and rejoice all their last day more than ever they did before. Now I too, as I believe, am a fellow-servant of the swans, and consecrated to the service of the same god ; I have received from my master a prophetic gift equal to theirs, and quit life as cheerfully as they. Nay, so far as this is concerned, you must say what you will, ask what questions you please, — as long as the officers of justice allow it.'

"'That is well,' replied Simmias ; 'then I will tell you my difficulty, and Cebes shall tell you what is his objection to what has been said. For my own thought about such matters, Socrates, is perhaps the same as your own :—that although to have clear knowledge about such matters as these in this present life is very difficult, if not impossible; still, not to test common opinions in every way, with zeal that is wearied by nothing short of a thorough examination, would be arrant cowardice : as I hold that to one end we must attain in this study—either we must be taught the truth, or we must seek and find it ; or if we cannot do this, we must take at least the best and hardest to disprove of human doctrines, and make this a raft whereon to accomplish the perilous voyage of life—unless indeed we can find some divine doctrine which will make a craft wherein to sail with more safety and less peril.'"

After Socrates has heard and answered Simmias'

and Cebes' objections (the latter contending that while the argument has proved that the soul is longer-lived than the body, actual immortality has yet to be established), the "divine doctrine" of his reply is crowned by a word-picture of the universe and the state of the dead.

"'This, then, is my conviction :—If the earth is a spherical body poised in mid heaven, it has no need of air or any such force to save it from falling, as the unbroken equality of all the circles of heaven and its own equilibrium are quite sufficient to support it. A perfectly-balanced body forming the centre of an unbroken circle will not be susceptible of the least inclination in any direction, but being equidistant from all parts of the circle will remain stationary. Such is the first article of my creed. Secondly: I believe this earth to be a very large body, of which we who dwell between the Phasis and the Pillars of Heracles inhabit only a tiny fraction ; we live round our sea like ants or frogs round a pond ; and there are many similar regions inhabited by numbers of other beings like ourselves. All over the earth there are hollows of infinite variety in shape and size, in which water and mist and vapour have collected ; while the real earth

lies pure and unsullied, with the heavens naked
around it. In this heaven the celestial bodies
move; and it is this which most of our teachers
call ether or upper air: our waters and our atmosphere are but its impurities, and settle like a
sediment into the cavities of the earth. Now we
men are under the mistaken impression that we
live on the upper regions of earth, whereas we
really dwell in its hollows. It is just as if some
inhabitant of the bottom of the sea were to believe
that he lived on its surface, and that the sea was
the sky because its water was the medium through
which he saw the sun and stars; and we must
suppose, moreover, that he is so awkward and feeble
that he has never made his way to the top, and
emerged and descried the superior beauty and
purity of the upper world, and that no one has ever
told him of such a sight. That is (I take it) what
has happened to us: we live in a cavity, yet
imagine that we inhabit the heights; we call our
lower atmosphere the firmament of heaven, and
think that it is in that atmosphere that the celestial
bodies move; the reason being, that our awkward-
ness and feebleness prevent us from making our
way up to the surface of the lower air. If one
could but mount or fly up to the highest levels, he

would emerge and see the world above, just as fish
put their heads out of the water and see the
world below; and if he were strong enough to bear
the sight he would recognise that there is the true
heaven, the true light, the true earth. For our
earth, with the stones and all that surrounds us here,
is all marred by corruption and corrosion, just as
everything in the sea is marred by the salt water ;
in the sea nothing of any account grows, or comes
(as one may say) to perfection, but even where
there is a stable bottom it is all rocky clefts and
sand and mud and slough unfathomable—not to be
compared with the fair sights of this earth. And
so it would appear that between the upper world
and ours there is a still greater difference. If
besides this you would have me tell you a beautiful
fable, it is well worth your while, Simmias, to
hear of those parts of earth which lie nearest to
heaven.

"'We are told, then, that the earth which I speak
of, viewed from above, resembles those balls which
are made of twelve leather strips ; like them, it is
mapped out into various colours, of which the
colours used by our painters are, as it were, sym-
bols.   There, the whole surface of the earth is
similarly coloured, but with brighter and purer

hues than ours ; part of it is a marvellously beautiful purple ; part shines like gold ; some of it is
white, and whiter than chalk or snow; and the
rest displays a variety of colours in like manner,
more numerous and more beautiful than any
known to us ; for even the cavities which I have
described, full as they are of water and vapour,
reflect the surrounding tints so as to present an
appearance of colour, and thus the impression produced is of one variegated surface. Such is its
aspect ; and every thing that grows there, be it
tree, flower, or fruit, is of corresponding beauty.
Nay, the mountains and stones possess a propor-
tionately greater smoothness and transparency and
brilliancy of colouring ; they are like to or more
beautiful than our precious stones, such as jasper,
cornelian, and emerald, which are in fact fragments
of them.   This is because the stones there are pure
and unblemished, there being no masses of matter
such as have collected here to wear and corrode
them with brine and rot—for it is these agencies
which render our stones and earth and plants
and animals ugly and sickly.   And it is not only
such as these with which the earth there is ap-
parelled, but gold and silver too, and the other
precious metals, great quantities of which lie in

full view all over the ground ; so that happy indeed is he who beholds such a spectacle. Human
beings exist there, as well as other living creatures ; some dwell inland, some on the margin of
the atmosphere ; in short, the lower air and the
ether stand to them in the same stead respectively
as water and the lower air do to us. Their seasons
are so tempered that they know no sickness and
are far longer-lived than we, while all their senses,
sight, hearing, and smell, are as much clearer than
ours as air is clearer than water and ether than
air.   Moreover, there are shrines and temples,
wherein the gods do truly dwell ; men hear their
voices and oracles, perceive their presence, and
have full communion with them ; they see the
real sun, and the real moon and stars ; and in all
respects enjoy a similar degree of blessedness.

   " ' Such is the earth as a whole, and such are its
surroundings.   Now there are numerous places all
over the sphere where its surface is depressed ;
some of these cavities are both deeper and wider
than that in which we live ; some are deeper and
narrower at the top than ours, while some again
are broader and shallower. All these are connected with each other by a system of subterranean
channels and passages of greater or less width.

Backwards and forwards through these passages,
filling the hollows like bowls, hot and cold streams
of enormous length flow unceasingly beneath the
earth ; great rivers of fire too, and many mud-
streams more or less fluid, like those that precede
the lava-flow of Etna, or like the lava itself.
These substances fill whatever hollow is in turn
approached by the tide in its circuit. All of these
are caused to ebb and flow upwards and downwards by an oscillating force present in the earth,
which again is the result of the conditions which I
will describe. The largest cavity of all penetrates
right through the whole of the earth ; it is that to
which Homer alludes in the line—

> "Far away under the earth, in the deepest of all her
> abysses,"

and is called by him elsewhere, as well as by many
other poets, Tartarus. All the rivers flow into
and out of this chasm, altering their several
natures according to that of the ground through
which they run. The reason of this universal
influx and efflux is that the fluid matter in Tartarus, having no bottom or resting-place, heaves
and surges up and down, and the accompanying
vapour and air follow its motions in whatever
direction it tends,—whether towards our side of

the world or the contrary part,—rising and falling
with the flood in a manner similar to the expulsion
and indrawing of the breath, and causing thereby
terrible and irresistible winds as it goes to and fro.
Whenever the impetus of the flood has carried it
into the so-called lower regions, it comes pouring
through the earth into the parts about the streams
which are there, filling them as with water pumped
into a bucket; and whenever it leaves those regions
and comes rushing back to our side, it fills the
nearer parts of the abyss, so that the waters overflow and course off through their subterranean
channels, until, as they arrive at their several des-
tinations, they form seas, lakes, rivers, and wells.
Thence they once more plunge underground, and
making a wider or narrower circuit past places of
greater or lesser importance, fall again into Tartarus, always at a place below the point of their
issue, but some farther down than others. Some
streams make their exit and entrance on opposite
sides, and others on the same side; while sometimes
they make a complete circuit, and winding round
the earth in one or more snake-like gyrations, fall
again into the abyss at the lowest point possible.
They cannot descend in either direction beyond
the centre, for from whichever quarter the streams

come, the incline of the opposite side is against
farther progress. These streams are many and
great, and of infinite variety, and among them are
four in especial. The largest is that which we call
Ocean ; it is the outermost of all, and encircles
the earth. The second, Acheron, emerges at an
opposite point to Ocean, and runs in a contrary
direction ; among the many desolate regions
which it traverses, it comes by an underground
course to the Acherusian lake, at the place where
the souls of most of the dead come and abide for
their appointed times, till after a shorter or a
longer period they are sent forth again to be born
into life. The third river issues between the two
first, and not far from its outfall descends into a
wide tract of burning fire, where it broadens into a
lake of boiling mud and water, larger than our
sea ; thence it describes a circle, flowing with a
turbid and muddy current, and as it winds approaches in course of time, without joining, the
Acherusian lake ; then, after many subterranean
windings, it falls into a lower part of Tartarus.
This is the river called Pyriphlegethon, jets from
which are emitted by all the volcanic streams in
the world. The fourth emerges opposite to the
third, and comes first to a wild and dreadful region

(so it is said) of a dull blue colour throughout; this is known as the Stygian land, and the lake formed by the outfall of the river is called Styx. Flowing into this lake, and thereby receiving certain strange properties into its waters, the stream plunges underground and goes winding round in a contrary direction to Pyriphlegethon, which it meets and passes near the Acherusian lake; and, like the third river, this too mingles its waters with no others, but circles round till it falls into Tartarus at the opposite side to Pyriphlegethon. Poets call it Cocytus.

"'Such is the state of that world. Now on the arrival of the dead at the place whither each is conducted by his guiding genius, judgment is first passed on those who have lived a good and holy life and those who have not. Then, as many as are judged to have lived in a mean state between good and evil betake themselves to the river Acheron, where they embark in what vessels they have for transport and are thus carried to the lake; there they dwell, and get quit of their several offences by purgation and punishment of the wrong that they have done, and for his good deeds each receives such honours as he deserves. But for those who are judged incurable, by reason of the heinousness of their crimes, whether they have

P

committed many grievous acts of sacrilege, or slain many men in despite of justice and law, or done any such-like deeds,—these are justly doomed to be cast into Tartarus, whence they never come out again. Those who have greatly sinned, yet not past atonement—done violence in anger to parents or committed a murder, yet lived thereafter a life of repentance—must indeed be thrown into the abyss; yet when they have remained therein for a twelvemonth the surge casts them all out, the murderer by way of the stream Cocytus, and the wronger of parents by Pyriphlegethon. And when the stream is carrying him past the Acherusian Lake, he calls aloud on those whom he has slain or maltreated, and then implores and entreats them to suffer him to come forth from the stream into the lake, and to receive him there. If he can prevail with them he leaves the stream and is no more afflicted; but if he cannot, he is borne back into Tartarus, and thence again into the river, and is thus dealt with till he has prevailed with the victims of his crime: such is the doom appointed by his judges. But if any are declared to have lived a life of especial goodness, these are they whose departure from our earthly regions is, as it were, a release and escape from a prison; and they ascend to the unsullied abodes and dwell on the high places of the earth. Among them, those who have sufficiently purified themselves by true knowledge are freed from their bodies and live thus eternally, and attain to abodes yet fairer than the rest, of which the full description were no light task, and would be longer than time at present permits.

" 'Looking, then, to all that I have set forth, we should use all diligence to live a life of goodness and wisdom; for fair is the prize, and high the hope.'

" Having thus spoken he rose and went into another room to wash; Crito followed him, bidding me wait. We therefore stayed where we were, now discussing and reviewing what had been said, and now enlarging on the greatness of the misfortune which had befallen us; for we thought it was as if we had lost a father—our future state must be no better than that of orphans. When Socrates had finished washing and his children had been brought to him—he had three boys, two little and one big—and the women of his house had also come, he talked with them in Crito's presence, giving them such charges as he wished; then he sent the women and children

away and came to join us. It was by this time
near sunset; for he had passed a long time in
the inner room. So he sat there after his bath;
but before many words had passed between us
the servant of the Eleven entered and came up
to him. 'Socrates,' said he, 'I can never com-
plain of you as I do of others, that they burst
into angry imprecations against me when I obey
authority and bid them drink the poison. You,
on the other hand, have lately proved yourself in
every respect the kindliest and gentlest and best
of all who ever came here; and now I am sure it
is not I but my masters whom you will blame;
for you know where the fault lies. So now, as
you know what my message is, take my best
wishes and try to bear your fate as readily as
may be.' With that he broke into weeping and
turned to go. Socrates looked up at him and
said, 'Do you take my best wishes too; I will
do your bidding.' Turning to us, 'Is he not,'
says he, 'a well-mannered fellow? it was so all
the time—he would be visiting me, and sometimes
talking, showing himself the best of men; and
now, how kind it is in him to weep for me! Well,
Crito, let us do as he says, and have the poison
brought, if it is ground yet; or if not, let the fellow

grind it.' 'Nay, Socrates,' said Crito, 'the sun
is surely still on the mountains, and not yet set.
Besides, I know that some people, after receiving
notice of death, do not take the poison till quite
late, after eating and drinking their fill, and sometimes enjoying such society as they desire. Do
not be in a hurry ; there is still time enough.'
'It is quite natural,' replied Socrates, 'that those
persons whom you speak of should act as they
do ; they think to gain by their conduct; and it is
equally natural that I should not do so, for I am
sure I gain nothing by putting off the draught, and
should only be a laughing-stock to myself for being
a miser of my life when there is none of it left.
Nay,' said he, 'do nothing else but what I tell you.'

"At this Crito beckoned to the slave, as he stood
near. The servant then went out, and returned
after a considerable time with the man who was to
administer the poison, carrying it ready ground
in a cup. When Socrates saw the fellow, he said,
'Well, sir, what am I to do ? you understand these
things.' 'Just drink,' said the other, 'and then
walk about till your legs feel heavy; after that lie
down ; so it will work of itself.' At the same time
he gave Socrates the cup. He took it very quietly
without a tremor, or change of colour or look.

Then fixing his eyes on the fellow in his usual way, 'How say you,' he asked, 'as to using some of the potion for a libation? is it lawful or not?' On being told that 'they only ground so much as was thought a sufficient draught,' 'I understand,' said he; 'but it is lawful and necessary, I suppose, to pray to the gods that I may be fortunate in changing my home for the other world: so I do pray, and so may it be.' With that he put the cup to his lips, and drank it off calmly and easily.

"Up to this point most of us had been tolerably well able to restrain our tears; but when we saw him drink and finish the draught, we could do so no longer: for my own part I could not help weeping copiously, so I covered my face and lamented my hard fate with tears—not his lot, but my own—when I thought of the good comrade I had lost. Crito had already risen and gone out before this, unable to restrain his emotion; and Apollodorus, who had never ceased weeping all through the preceding hours, now burst into such a torrent of tears and complaints that all present were deeply moved—all but Socrates himself. All that *he* said was, 'This is strange conduct. Why, it was for this I sent the women away, that they might not so misbehave themselves. I have heard

that a man should die in peace.   Nay, be still and
patient!'   This made us ashamed, and we checked
our tears.   Socrates then walked about, and when
he said his legs felt heavy, lay down on his back,
according   to   the   man's   directions.   He   who
administered   the   poison   touched   him,   and
presently examined his hands and feet; then he
pinched Socrates' foot hard and asked if he felt it.
Socrates said, 'No.'   After this he did the same to
the shins, and so gradually ascending made it
clear to us that the body was becoming numb and
rigid ; touching it, in fact, himself, and telling us
that it would be all over as soon as the heart was
reached.   Now when the chill reached as far as the
parts about the abdomen, Socrates uncovered his
face—for it had been concealed—and uttered his
last words: 'Crito, I owe a cock to Asclepius.
Pay the debt; do not forget it.'   'It shall be
done,' said Crito ; 'have you any other command?'
But to this question Socrates made no answer.
Presently he stirred, and on the man's uncovering
the face we saw that the eyes were fixed.   Crito
then closed the mouth and eyelids.

" Thus died our comrade,—who, in our judgment,
was the best man known to us, and the wisest and
justest known to the world."

CHAPTER XI

THE STORY OF ER

No view of Socrates, however superficial, can omit some notice of the μῦθοι or stories which form a considerable part of several of the Platonic dialogues. How far they are really Socratic, it is impossible to decide. They may be Plato's altogether. They may be the pupil's reminiscences of apologues sketched or suggested by his master. But there is nothing inherently improbable in the presumption that the addition of some such narrative to the dialogue was a part of the Socratic method; in fact, the balance of probability is in its favour. Monologues belonged to the stock-in-trade of professional teachers, such as Protagoras, who in fact can hardly be persuaded to join in a discussion where he himself is not allowed to be in possession of the house for an unlimited time. In the *Memorabilia* Socrates closes a controversy by repeating the story of the Choice of Heracles. Altogether, external evidence is rather in favour of the myth being attributable to Socrates himself; and the moral of three among them at least is precisely that which—looking to the general consensus of evidence as to the principles which are to be associated with his name—we should expect Socrates to draw.

These three, the greatest of the Platonic myths, form part of the dialogues entitled *Gorgias*, *Phaedo*, and *Republic;* and they are concerned with the same subject—the Last Judgment, and the world beyond the grave. In them is contained the germ of those beliefs which have formed the most important part of the creed of civilisation as to a future state. Here we see Nirvana, there Purgatory—the eternal Heaven of the Christian, the metempsychosis of the Pythagorean. The "savage men of fiery aspect" who carry off the bad in the *Republic* are the devils of the mediæval mystery play. The Tartarus of the *Phaedo* is the lake that burneth with fire and brimstone. Much of the similarity between the Platonic and later pictures is, of course, the result of direct imitation; for instance, Virgil, the prince and pattern of plagiarists, has copied from all the

three myths. His *Inferno* is a cento of details
drawn not only from Homer's Νεκυΐα, but from
the *Phaedo*, the *Republic*, and the *Gorgias*.

Obviously, we cannot suppose that either
Socrates or Plato regarded these apologues as
in any sense representing a sincere creed. The
apparatus and adornment of each particular myth
may be due to the desire of inculcating some
moral appropriate to the particular dialogue, or
to many reasons unknown or obscure to us. In-
consistencies abound; for instance, in the *Republic* all the souls except those of the incurably
bad are subject to transmigration; while in the
Phaedo it is only those who have been neither
good nor bad wholly, and the forgiven sinners,
who are destined once more to be born into life.
The "purgatory" of the *Phaedo* is altogether
different from that of the *Republic:* in the former
the soul is carried to and fro by subterranean
currents; in the latter the expiation consists in
a thousand years' underground journey. In one
dialogue metempsychosis necessarily precludes any
eternal state. In another the souls of the just
live for ever in bliss. But all three myths coin-
cide in this—there is a heaven, there is a hell,
and there is a purgatory. In the *Phaedo*, where

the account of the several conditions is most
minutely worked out, there are five states : hell ;
the state of great sinners who have repented in
life ; the state of the moderately good ; the state
of the good ; the state of those who add to their
goodness " philosophy." In the *Gorgias* the object
is to show that success in this world may be ill-
success in the next. Socrates is concerned to
prove in the *Phaedo* that the soul's severance from
the body may be an actual benefit. In the myth
of Er, the messenger from the other world has
seen nothing less than the whole government of
the Universe and the whole destiny of man. But
in all the moral is the same : it is that undoubtedly
Socratic doctrine that things are not in reality
what they seem to us here in life ; and that well-
doing is in the long run more profitable than evil-
doing.

Several myths have been already translated. The
myth which closes the *Republic* runs as follows :

" Well," I said, " this is no Adventure of Odysseus which I will relate to you, but the adventures
of a brave Pamphylian, Er the son of Armenius.
He was slain in battle ; and although the dead
were not taken up for ten days, and the rest of

them were corrupt, he was found yet untainted, and brought home and laid on the pyre for his funeral; where after twelve days he came to life again, and recounted what he had seen in the other world. This was his story:—As soon as his soul had gone forth from the body, it journeyed in a great company, till they came to a certain ghostly place, where were two clefts in the earth near to each other, and two others over against them above in the heaven. Between these sat judges, who when they had given judgment, bade the righteous depart by the way that led to the right and upward through the heaven, having first fastened on them in front tokens of the judgment given,—while the unrighteous were bidden to take the left hand and downward way, they too wearing behind them marks declaring their deeds. But when Er approached, the judges said that he must bear to mankind the message of what befell in that other state, and they counselled him to listen and look well to all that was to be seen and heard. Then he saw how the souls, when sentence had been pronounced upon them, were one way departing by two of those clefts,—one in heaven and one on earth,—and how they were returning by way of the other two: here coming up from the earth covered with grime and dust, and there descending from the heaven pure and spotless. And ever as they came they seemed like travellers after a long journey, and glad they were to depart into the meadow hard by, where they encamped as at a festal gathering; and there those that were known to each other exchanged greetings, and the souls that had come from the earth would ask the others how they had fared on their way, and those that came from the heaven inquired in like manner. Some told their tale with lamentation and weeping, remembering all the sufferings and sights of their journey beneath the earth—and the length of that journey was one thousand years,—and those newly come from the heaven spoke of joys and scenes beautiful beyond expression. Most of what was said would take long to relate; but the sum of this story (so said Er) was this :—That each had been punished in turn for every wrong he had done and every victim of the wrong, for each offence paying tenfold, that is, once in every century,—such being deemed to be the length of human life,—so that the penalty paid might be ten times as great as the wrong. So, whosoever had put many to death, or betrayed cities or armies into slavery, or aided to bring about any

other calamity, had received for each sin tenfold
affliction ; and again, for all good deeds done, and
for justice and holiness, due requital was made in
like manner. Er said, too, certain things of no
great import concerning the fate of children dead
a short while after birth. But the wages of irreverence or reverence shown to gods and parents, and
of murder of kinsfolk, were, as he related, greater
than all. One in his presence asked of another,
Where is the great Ardiaeus ? Now Ardiaeus had
been despot of a certain Pamphylian city one thousand years before that time, and, as it was reported,
had put his aged father and his elder brother to
death, and done many other unholy deeds. He
then that was questioned, replied, 'He has not come
hither, nor will he come. That indeed was one of
the terrible sights which we saw : when the rest of
our travail was accomplished and we were near the
mouth of the pit and like to come up, suddenly
we saw Ardiaeus with others, tyrants for the most
part, though there were with them some great
sinners of lower estate. Now, as these thought to
ascend, the mouth of the pit suffered them not,
but uttered a roar whenever any that were either
so incurably wicked or had not paid the full
penalty essayed to come up. Then ' (he said)

'certain savage men of fiery aspect, standing hard by and hearing the voice, seized and led away some of that company; but Ardiaeus and others they bound hand and foot and head, and cast them down and flayed them with scourges, and then dragged them off beside the way, carding them on thorns, declaring to all who passed by wherefore they endured this punishment, and to what purpose they were being carried away to be hurled into the nether abyss. Of the many and divers terrors we had encountered (said he) none was equal to this: for each of us feared lest he should hear that roaring when he was going up, and right glad he was to pass forth when the voice was not uttered.' Such, said Er, were the dooms and penalties, and the rewards were apportioned in like fashion.

"Now when the souls in the meadow had stayed each for seven days, on the eighth they must rise and journey on; and after four days they came to a place whence they could see below them a pillar of light stretching straight downwards full across heaven and earth, most like a rainbow, but brighter and purer in aspect. To this they came after one day's journey farther; when they saw the ends of the chains of heaven stretching therefrom, and

made fast midway down the column of light—for
this light was the bond that holds together the
whole circumference of heaven, like the girder of a
trireme. And to the ends of the chains was
fastened the spindle of necessity, whereby all the
spheres revolve. Its stalk and hook were of adamant, and its whorl of adamant and other substances combined. The whorl was of the ordinary
shape, such as we see. But, for its construction,
we must infer from the story that it resembled
one large whorl with all the interior scooped out
hollow, and containing seven other whorls of less
and less circumference adapted to its shape, like
those boxes that are made to fit into each other;
for the whorls were eight in all, placed one within
the other, so that the edges of the eight concentric
circles were visible from above, and formed the
continuous surface of a single whorl having the
stalk for centre, which ran right through the middle
of the eighth. The widest rim was that of the
first and outer whorl, the breadth then gradually
decreasing through the sixth, fourth, eighth,
seventh, fifth and third, down to the second, which
was narrowest of all. Moreover, the rim of the
largest whorl was varied in colour, while that of
the seventh was the brightest, and that of the

eighth took its colour from the reflected light of
the seventh; the second and fifth were like each
other, and yellower than those before named; the
third was the whitest of all, the fourth reddish, and
the sixth next in whiteness to the third. The
whole spindle was turning with a regular circling
motion; but while the whole revolved one way,
the seven inner rings moved slowly in the reverse
direction, the eighth turning most rapidly, and
next at an equal rate the seventh, sixth, and fifth;
the reverse movement of the fourth appeared to
be slower still, next that of the third, while the
second was slowest of all. The spindle revolved
on the knees of Necessity. And aloft, on each
of the circles, stood a siren, moving round with its
motion, uttering still the same sound—one single
note, so that the eight notes composed one melody.
Moreover, there were three thrones set at equal
distances round the spindle, whereon sat three
that wore white raiment and fillets on their heads:
these were Fates, the daughters of Necessity—
Lachesis, Clotho, and Atropos: and they chanted
in unison with the sirens' melody, Lachesis the song
of the past, Clotho of the present, and Atropos
of the future; and ever and anon Clotho would lay
her right hand on the outer ring of the spindle and

help its turning, while Atropos did in like manner
to the inner rings, and Lachesis touched with
either hand outer and inner rings in turn.

"So when the souls came there they must
straightway go before Lachesis. Then one who
interpreted her will, first marshalled them in order,
and then, taking from Lachesis' knees where they
lay lots and samples of divers lives, he mounted
a high pulpit and said : 'These are the words of
Lachesis, the virgin daughter of Necessity. Souls,
creatures of a day ! now beginneth another span of
mortality. Ye shall choose your genius, not by your
genius be chosen. Let him to whom the lot gives
the first place, first choose that life wherewith
he needs must dwell. But virtue knows no con-
straint ; of which, as he honoureth it or dishonour-
eth, he shall in greater or less measure partake.
Be the choice on the chooser's head ; blame not
God therefore !' Having thus spoken he cast the
lots among the multitude, and each save Er alone—
for he was forbidden—took up the lot that fell near
him ; and the soul that took it up saw there what
place it assigned him in the choosing. After this
the interpreter set on the ground before them the
samples of divers lives; and these were of all kinds,
and far more numerous than the souls present.

There were all the lives of men and of all living creatures—princedoms, some of lifelong duration, some untimely cut short and ending in penury, exile, and beggary; lives of men honoured or unhonoured, whether for an outward show of beauty and strength and might in contending, or for their lineage and the excellence of their forefathers: and lives of women likewise. There was no fixed state of soul for choice, because the soul must needs change according to the life it chose; but to all else save this were united destinies of wealth and penury, sickness and health, and sometimes a mingling of all. In this choice then, as it would seem, lies all our danger; and therefore it is that there is one knowledge which each of us must with especial care study and learn, even to the neglect of all else—the knowledge where he may find a teacher who will make him a master of the science of distinguishing good and bad ways of life and so choosing always and everywhere the best way possible, because he can calculate how far the combination or division of all the destinies we have mentioned affects excellence of living; who will teach him how, with a different state of the soul, different good and evil results follow from the unison of beauty with poverty or wealth; and what effect is produced by the combination of inherent gifts or acquired attributes, such as birth mean and noble, lowly and sovereign station, strength, weakness, quickness, and dullness : so that the learner may be able to reason in his choice from all these premises, and so distinguish the worse and the better life with a single eye to his soul's welfare and an absolute neglect of all besides : deeming that life the worst which will lead his soul towards injustice, and that the better which will lead her towards justice ; for we have seen that this is the best way of choosing whether in life or in death. This opinion he must hold with a grasp of steel when he departs to the other world ; thus will he not be dazzled by wealth and such-like evils, and so by blindly choosing such a destiny as the tyrant's inflict much incurable mischief on others and suffer yet more himself ; but he will know how to choose here the middle path of life, and shun the excess and defect as far as may be, both in this life and all that which follows ; for this is the truest road to human happiness.

" Then (as the messenger from thence reported) the interpreter spoke thus : 'Even for the last comer, if he choose with judgment and live earnestly, lieth there no evil life, but such as may

well content him. Let neither the first be careless
in his choice, nor the last despair.' When he had
thus spoken, he to whom the first place was allotted
came and straightway chose the greatest of the
sovereignties ; and so foolish was he and greedy
that he 'chose without making full and sufficient
scrutiny, but he wist not how it was written in
that destiny that he should devour his own children
and suffer other ills ; so when he looked into it at
leisure, he bewailed and lamented his choice, and
forgot the interpreter's warning, blaming chance
and heaven and everything but himself for his
calamity. This man was one of those who had
come from heaven, and had lived his former life in
an ordered state, where he was virtuous not from
philosophy but from habit. It were true to say
that those who came from heaven were oftenest
thus deceived, because they were unschooled in
sorrows ; whereas those who came from the earth,
inasmuch as they had both themselves suffered
and seen others suffer, for the most part made
not their choice hastily; for which cause, as also
by reason of the chance of the lot, most souls
reversed the good or evil of their former state.
Yet if, when coming to the choice of an earthly
life, we could be sound philosophers and were

allotted places not among the last choosers, it seems likely from the reports of that other world that we have a good chance not only of happiness in this, but of journeying thither and back again, not by the rough path below the earth but by the smooth road of heaven.

" ' Now the spectacle (said Er) of the souls choosing their several lives was a sight well worth the seeing ; so pitiable was it and laughable, and so strange. For the most part, they chose as their old life's experience taught them.' He saw how because Orpheus had been slain by women, the soul once his hated all the sex, and chose the life of a swan, lest it should be conceived and born of a woman ; and how Thamyrus took the life of a nightingale; and how a swan chose instead of its own the life of a man, and other singing creatures did likewise. The soul that by lot came the twentieth chose the life of a lion; now this was the soul of Aias, son of Telamon, who shunned a human form because he remembered the adjudgment of Achilles' armour. The next soul was that of Agamemnon, and it likewise, hating men by reason of his evil fate, exchanged his life for an eagle's. To the soul of Atalanta had fallen a middle place in the throng ; who, seeing the glories

of an athlete's life, could not forbear choosing
them. Then the soul of Epeius, son of Panopeus,
was seen taking the estate of a craftswoman, and far
down among the last comers, the soul of Thersites
the buffoon, taking the life of an ape. Now the
lot had so chanced that last of all the soul of
Odysseus came to the choosing, and that soul—for
ambition was quenched in it by the remembrance
of its former toils—sought long and diligently for
a life of idle privacy ; and when after much searching one such was found, which lay neglected by all
the rest, gladly took it, saying, ' I would have done
the same had the lot given me the first choice.'
And the souls of beasts besides passed, some
into men and some into beasts again, the bad into
fierce and the good into gentle creatures, undergoing every form of change. So when all the
souls had chosen their lives in the allotted order,
they came one after another before Lachesis ; and
she sent with each the genius he had chosen, to be
his guardian through life and fulfil the chosen destiny. This genius first led the soul under the
hand of Clotho, and the revolution of her whirling
spindle, so as to ratify the fate it had selected as
by lot ordained ; having touched this, it was led
to where Atropos spun, whereby the genius made

the destiny irreversible ; and thence the soul went
without turning back under the throne of Necessity.   And when it and all the rest had passed
beneath that throne, they all journeyed together to
the plain of Oblivion, through a land of exceeding
sultry and burning heat ; for all that place was
bare of trees and all else that grows from the
earth.   So when it was come to evening they
camped by the river of Forgetfulness, the water
whereof no vessel can hold.   Of this water all
must needs drink a measure, and they that were
not guarded by prudence drank immoderately; and
whoever had drunk of it, forgot all things.   Then
when they had lain down to rest, at midnight
came thunder and an earthquake, and on a sudden
the souls were borne darting upwards different
ways to their birth, like shooting stars.   For himself (said Er), he had been forbidden to drink of
the water ; yet how and what way he came to his
body he knew not ; only he looked up suddenly
and found himself at dawn lying on the pyre."

THE END.

[R. Clay & Sons, Ld., London & Bungay.

Issued in large crown 8vo., with Portraits on Copper.
Second Edition.

STUDIES IN MODERN MUSIC.

HECTOR BERLIOZ, ROBERT SCHUMANN, RICHARD WAGNER.

By W. H. HADOW, M.A., *Fellow of Worcester College, Oxon.*

"We have seldom read a book on musical subjects which has given us so much pleasure as this one, and we can sincerely recommend it to all who are interested in the art."—*Saturday Review.*

"It is a real relief, amid the rambling and slipshod effusions which constitute the bulk of musical *belles lettres*, to encounter such a volume as these 'Studies in Modern Music,' by Mr. W. H. Hadow. Mr. Hadow is himself a musician of no mean attainments ; but there is no parade of technical knowledge in his book. He writes like a scholar and a gentleman, his style is felicitous and his critical attitude at once sane and generous."—*Graphic.*

"He writes with striking thoughtfulness and breadth of view, so that his essays may be read with much interest by musicians. It is a remarkable book, because, unlike the majority of musical treatises by amateurs, it is full of truth and common-sense."—*Athenæum.*

"The essay on musical criticism is well worth anybody's reading; its general tendency is to extend the basis of modern criticism, commensurably with the larger and wider scope of modern music, to establish standards of musical value by which modern works can be more justly measured than by the pedantic misapplication of once valid rules. In his whole discourse on the subject Mr. Hadow gives evidence of immense common-sense, backed up by innate and cultivated artistic perception."—*Atlantic Monthly.*

BY THE SAME AUTHOR.

STUDIES IN MODERN MUSIC.

SECOND SERIES.

FREDERICK CHOPIN, ANTONIN DVORÁK, JOHANNES BRAHMS.
PRECEDED BY AN ESSAY ON MUSICAL FORM.

"The three biographies are charming : and in each case the author has something both true and new to say."—*National Observer.*

"The development of form is described with many brilliant touches and with complete grasp of the subject, and the book, which will probably be considered to be even better than the former work, is most heartily to be recommended to all who wish to attain the highest kind of enjoyment of the best music."—*Times.*

"Highly finished portraits are presented of the three modern masters named, and the articles are distinguished by the same musicianly knowledge and felicity of expression as those in the earlier book."—*Athenæum.*

"The amount of labour and research condensed into these pages is really remarkable."—*Musical Times.*

"There is not a word either in the historical or exegetical portions of Mr. Hadow's work which will not furnish agreeable suggestion to the casual reader, and satisfaction to the student."—*St. James's Gazette.*

LONDON : SEELEY AND CO., LIMITED, ESSEX ST., STRAND.

NEW AND CHEAPER EDITIONS OF SELECTED WORKS BY P. G. HAMERTON.

THE LIFE OF J. M. W. TURNER, R.A.

Illustrated with an entirely new set of illustrations. Large crown 8vo., cloth.

"A really notable piece of biography."—*Vanity Fair.*
"A real help to all who try to appreciate the genius of the great landscape painter."—*Pall Mall Gazette.*

PARIS IN OLD AND PRESENT TIMES.

With many illustrations. Large crown 8vo., cloth.

"To those who know what value to set on delicate and appreciative criticism, a genuine love of art and good literary style, we cordially commend this book."
—*Saturday Review.*

ROUND MY HOUSE. Notes of Rural Life in France in Peace and War.

Crown 8vo., cloth.

"Mr. Hamerton has given us the rare treat of an intellectual surprise. We open his book expecting a pleasant entertainment, and then find a theme of profound interest treated with masterly skill by a man of known ability. On laying down his book we know France as we never knew it before."—*Spectator.*

* THE SYLVAN YEAR. Leaves from the Note-book of Raoul Dubois.

With eight etchings. Crown 8vo., cloth.

"Few men with similar tastes will read these pages without extreme satisfaction."—*Athenæum.*

* CHAPTERS ON ANIMALS.

With eight etchings. Crown 8vo., cloth.

"An interesting book from a true lover and observer of animals."—*Standard.*

* *Editions of these two books on larger paper with twenty etchings are still published.*

LONDON: SEELEY & CO., LIMITED, ESSEX ST., STRAND.

EIGHTEENTH CENTURY WRITERS

DEAN SWIFT: LIFE AND WRITINGS. By GERALD MORI-
ARTY, Balliol College, Oxford. With Nine Portraits, after LELY, KNEL-
LER, etc. 7s. 6d. ; large paper copies (150 only), 21s.

'Mr. Moriarty is to be heartily congratulated upon having produced an extremely sound
and satisfactory little book.'—*National Observer.*

HORACE WALPOLE AND HIS WORLD. Select Passages
from his Letters. With Eight Copper-plates, after Sir JOSHUA REYNOLDS
and THOMAS LAWRENCE. Second Edition. Crown 8vo. 7s. 6d.,
cloth.

' A compact representative selection, with just enough connecting text to make it read con-
secutively, with a pleasantly-written introduction.'—*Athenæum.*

Also cheap edition. Price 3s. 6d.

FANNY BURNEY AND HER FRIENDS. Select Passages
from her Diary. Edited by L. B. SEELEY, M.A., late Fellow of Trinity
College, Cambridge. With Nine Portraits on Copper, after REYNOLDS,
GAINSBOROUGH, COPLEY, and WEST. Third Edition. 7s. 6d., cloth.

'The charm of the volume is heightened by nine illustrations of some of the master-pieces
of English art, and it would not be possible to find a more captivating present for any one
beginning to appreciate the characters of the last century.'—*Academy.*

Also cheap edition. Price 3s. 6d.

MRS. THRALE, AFTERWARDS MRS. PIOZZI. By L. B.
SEELEY, M.A., late Fellow of Trinity College, Cambridge. With Nine
Portraits on Copper, after HOGARTH, REYNOLDS, ZOFFANY, and others.
7s. 6d., cloth.

'This sketch is better worth having than the autobiography, for it is infinitely the more
complete and satisfying.'—*Globe.*

LADY MARY WORTLEY MONTAGU. By ARTHUR R.
ROPES, M.A., sometime Fellow of King's College, Cambridge. With
Nine Portraits, after Sir GODFREY KNELLER, etc. 7s. 6d.; large paper
copies (150 only), net 21s.

'Embellished as it is with a number of excellent plates, we cannot imagine a more welcome
or delightful present.'—*National Observer.*

SIR JOSHUA REYNOLDS AND THE ROYAL ACADEMY.
By CLAUDE PHILLIPS. With Nine Plates after the Artist's Pictures. Price
7s. 6d., cloth ; large paper copies, 21s.

'Mr. Phillips writes with knowledge, insight, and original inspiration—full of accurate
information and sound criticism.'—*Times.*

LONDON : SEELEY & CO., LIMITED, ESSEX ST., STRAND.

POPULAR SCIENCE

RADIANT SUNS. A Sequel to 'Sun, Moon, and Stars.' By A. GIBERNE. With Illustrations. Crown 8vo, cloth. Price 5*s*.

SUN, MOON, AND STARS. A Book on Astronomy for Beginners. By A. GIBERNE. With Illustrations. Twenty-first Thousand. Crown 8vo, cloth. Price 5*s*.

" One of the most fascinating books about astronomy ever written."—*Yorkshire Post.*

THE WORLD'S FOUNDATIONS: Geology for Beginners. By A. GIBERNE. With Illustrations. Sixth Thousand. Crown 8vo, cloth. Price 5*s*.

" The exposition is clear, the style simple and attractive."—*Spectator.*

THE OCEAN OF AIR. Meteorology for Beginners. By A. GIBERNE. With Illustrations. Fifth Thousand. Crown 8vo, cloth. Price 5*s*.

" Miss Giberne can be accurate without being formidable, and unites a keen sense of the difficulties of beginners to a full comprehension of the matter in hand."—*Saturday Review.*

AMONG THE STARS ; or, Wonderful Things in the Sky. By A. GIBERNE. With Illustrations. Seventh Thousand. Price 5*s*.

" We may safely predict that if it does not find the reader with a taste for astronomy it will leave him with one."—*Knowledge.*

THE GREAT WORLD'S FARM. How Nature grows her Crops. By SELINA GAYE. With a Preface by Prof. Boulger, and Sixteen Illustrations. Crown 8vo, cloth. Price 5*s*.

" A fascinating book of popular science."—*Times.*

THE STORY OF THE HILLS: A Popular Account of the Mountains and How they were Made. By the Rev. H. N. HUTCHINSON. With Sixteen Illustrations. Price 5*s*.

" Charmingly written, and beautifully illustrated."—*Yorkshire Post.*

LONDON : SEELEY & CO., LIMITED, ESSEX ST., STRAND.

Demy 8vo, Cloth.   Price 16s.

MADAME

Memoirs of Henrietta, Daughter of Charles I. and Duchess of Orleans.

By JULIA CARTWRIGHT (Mrs. H. Ady), Author of "Sacharissa."

With Two Portraits on Copper.

*** This Volume contains Ninety Unpublished Letters of Charles II.

" The book will certainly remain the standard authority on the subject for English readers."—*Athenæum.*

" Mrs. Ady has struck a vein of pure gold in her choice of the ladies of the 17th century."—*Guardian.*

Second Edition.   Demy 8vo.   Price 12s. 6d.

SACHARISSA

Some Account of Dorothy Sidney, Countess of Sunderland, her Family and Friends.

By JULIA CARTWRIGHT (Mrs. Henry Ady).

With Portrait after Vandyke.

" A thoroughly interesting book, with selections sometimes most felicitous."—*National Observer.*

" Mrs. Ady is much to be congratulated on this volume, in which she collects and gives to the world all that can be gathered together concerning the life and times of a most delightful and remarkable woman."—*Saturday Review.*

" Not only is it a valuable history of the great people of the time, but it is interesting reading throughout."—*Pall Mall.*

" In this attractive book a new light is cast on her great-hearted brother, Algernon Sidney, her famous son-in-law, Lord Halifax, and half the notables of that stormy age."—*Leeds Mercury.*

" We have nothing but praise for the way in which Miss Cartwright has done her work."—*Spectator.*

" Mrs. Ady has brought together an abundance of interesting details which make her volume delightful reading."—*Glasgow Herald.*

" This is a delightful book, and the story is pleasantly and sympathetically told. We are gratified to Miss Cartwright for thus preserving to us, in these pages, the memory of one who so fitly deserves our remembrance and our gratitude."—*Guardian.*

LONDON : SEELEY & CO., LIMITED, ESSEX ST., STRAND.

Issued in Demy 8vo.   Third Edition.   Price 12s. 6d.

LIFE AT THE ZOO

NOTES AND TRADITIONS OF THE REGENT'S PARK GARDENS.

By C. J. CORNISH.

Illustrated from Photographs by GAMBIER BOLTON.

OPINIONS OF THE PRESS.

" Mr. Cornish not only knows his dumb friends in Regent's Park institution and beyond its limits well enough to have acquired a profound understanding of their varying habits and peculiarities, but he is able to do the humour of the animal world an amount of justice such as it very rarely obtains . . . .   In its graver, as in its lighter portions, this absorbing work is without a single dull or superfluous line, and its value is not a little enhanced by the several beautiful reproductions of photographs by Mr. Gambier Bolton.   Alike for young people and for children of ' a larger growth,' the pleasure of a visit to the ' Zoo ' will be enhanced tenfold by a study of Mr. Cornish's equally diverting and instructive book."—*World.*

" Mr. Cornish is manifestly a keen lover of animals and a close observer of their habits and humours, and he records his observations in a very attractive fashion, genial in tone, curiously felicitous in description, and with frequent touches of quiet humour."—*Times.*

" He gives in short compass the results of long and patient observation, and in doing so displays to an envious degree the faculty of critical, but easy, exposition."—*Standard.*

" A charming series of sketches that form a pleasant medley for the lover of animals."—*Saturday Review.*

" A more companionable book than ' Life at the Zoo,' for a visitor to the great menagerie, we cannot imagine . . . .   Interesting, thoughtful, and teeming with acute and often minute observation, and the sympathy of a true naturalist."—*Spectator.*

" The articles on ' Animal Colouring,' ' Patterns on Living Animals,' ' The Speech of Monkeys,' ' The Temper of Animals,' and many others we might also mention, show startling insight and much originality.   Mr. Cornish writes well, and, if we mistake not, this should place him high in reputation amongst his brother naturalists."—*Black and White.*

" The book is beautifully illustrated, and one of the pleasantest introductions to popular natural history we have seen for some time."—*Daily Telegraph.*

" The book gives an account of the habits and nature of the inmates of the lordly prison-house in the Regent's Park, and of some of their past or future companions.   It is of absorbing interest throughout."—*Daily News.*

LONDON : SEELEY & CO., LIMITED, ESSEX ST., STRAND.

WILD ENGLAND OF TO-DAY

AND THE

WILD LIFE IN IT.

By C. J. CORNISH.

Illustrated with Original Drawings by LANCELOT SPEED, and from Photographs.

OPINIONS OF THE PRESS.

"Mr. Cornish has undoubtedly found his true vocation in describing his experiences of country scenery and animal life."—*Athenæum.*

"The chapters are instinct with a full appreciation of country life. . . . It is exceedingly well illustrated by drawings and photographs."—*Field.*

"The reader has delightful glimpses of the White Horse country, woods and fields in High Suffolk, Somersetshire coombs, and a Yorkshire fen."—*Daily News.*

"The whole of the sketches, while being quite popularly written, are scientifically accurate, without pretending to be permanent contributions to science. Charmingly indited, they remind one of the style and flavour of the late Richard Jeffries."—*Nature.*

"Each essay is so interesting that it is not easy to single any one out for special mention."—*National Observer.*

"The author is a naturalist who combines enviable lucidity of statement with much shrewd observation and a fund of quiet humour."—*Standard.*

"In reading these pages one seems to sniff the fresh sea-breezes, to hear the cries of the sea-bird, and the songs of the wood-bird, to be conscious of the murmuring stream and waving forest, and all the wild life that is therein."—*St. James's Gazette.*

LONDON: SEELEY & CO., LIMITED, ESSEX ST., STRAND.

EVENTS OF OUR OWN TIME

A Series of Volumes on the most Important Events of the last Half-Century, each containing 300 pages or more, in large 8vo, with Plans, Portraits, or other Illustrations, to be issued at intervals, cloth, price 5s.

Large paper copies (250 only) with Proofs of the Plates, cloth, 10s. 6d.

––––––––––

THE LIBERATION OF ITALY. By the COUNTESS MARTINENGO CESARESCO. With Four Portraits on Copper. Crown 8vo. Price 5s., cloth.

THE WAR IN THE CRIMEA. By General SIR EDWARD HAMLEY, K.C.B. With Five Maps and Plans, and Four Portraits on Copper. Fifth Edition. Crown 8vo. Price 5s., cloth.

THE INDIAN MUTINY OF 1857. By COLONEL MALLESON, C.S.I. With Three Plans, and Four Portraits on Copper. Sixth Edition. Crown 8vo. Price 5s., cloth.

THE AFGHAN WARS OF 1839-1842 AND 1878-80. By ARCHIBALD FORBES. With Five Maps and Plans, and Four Portraits on Copper. Second Edition. Crown 8vo. Price 5s., cloth.

THE REFOUNDING OF THE GERMAN EMPIRE. By COLONEL MALLESON, C.S.I. With Five Maps and Plans, and Four Portraits on Copper. Crown 8vo. Price 5s., cloth.

*ACHIEVEMENTS IN ENGINEERING DURING THE LAST HALF-CENTURY. By Professor VERNON HARCOURT. With many Illustrations. Crown 8vo. Price 5s., cloth.

*THE DEVELOPMENT OF NAVIES DURING THE LAST HALF-CENTURY. By Captain EARDLEY WILMOT, R.N. With Illustrations and Plans. Crown 8vo. Price 5s., cloth.

* Of Volumes so marked there are no Large Paper Editions.

––––––––––

LONDON : SEELEY & CO., LIMITED, ESSEX ST., STRAND.

BY THE REV. A. J. CHURCH

THE FALL OF ATHENS. A Tale of the Peloponnesian War.
With Sixteen Illustrations. Large Crown 8vo. Price 5s., cloth.

STORIES FROM THE GREEK COMEDIANS. With Sixteen
Coloured Illustrations. Price 5s., cloth.

'The broad humour of Aristophanes is most effectively given in this little book, and the
flashes of brilliant irony not less vividly.'—*Spectator.*

THE STORY OF THE ILIAD. With Coloured Illustrations.
Crown 8vo. Price 5s., cloth.

THE STORY OF THE ODYSSEY. With Coloured Illustrations. Crown 8vo. Price 5s., cloth.

'One of the most beautiful pieces of prose in the English language, as well as one which
gives a better notion of Homer than any one, probably, of our many meritorious metrical and
rhymed versions.'—*Spectator.*

STORIES FROM HOMER. With Coloured Illustrations.
Twenty-second Thousand. Price 5s., cloth.

'A book which ought to become an English classic. It is full of the pure Homeric flavour.'
—*Spectator.*

STORIES FROM VIRGIL. With Coloured Illustrations.
Sixteenth Thousand. Price 5s., cloth.

'Superior to his "Stories from Homer," good as they were, and perhaps as perfect a
specimen of that peculiar form of translation as could be.'—*Times.*

STORIES FROM THE GREEK TRAGEDIANS. With
Coloured Illustrations. Tenth Thousand. Price 5s., cloth.

'Not only a pleasant and entertaining book for the fireside, but a storehouse of facts from
history to be of real service to them when they come to read a Greek play for themselves.'—
Standard.

STORIES OF THE EAST FROM HERODOTUS. With
Coloured Illustrations. Ninth Thousand. Price 5s., cloth.

'For a school prize a more suitable book will hardly be found.'—*Literary Churchman.*

**THE STORY OF THE PERSIAN WAR FROM HERO-
DOTUS.** With Coloured Illustrations. Fifth Thousand. Price 5s.,
cloth.

'We are inclined to think this is the best volume of Professor Church's series since the
excellent "Stories from Homer."'—*Athenæum.*

STORIES FROM LIVY. With Coloured Illustrations. Sixth
Thousand. Price 5s., cloth.

'The lad who gets this book for a present will have got a genuine classical treasure.'—
Scotsman.

THE STORY OF THE LAST DAYS OF JERUSALEM
FROM JOSEPHUS. With Coloured Illustrations. Seventh Thousand.
Price 3s. 6d., cloth.

'The execution of this work has been performed with that judiciousness of selection and
felicity of language which have combined to raise Professor Church far above the fear of
rivalry.'—*Academy.*

LONDON : SEELEY & CO., LIMITED, ESSEX ST., STRAND.

BY THE REV. A. J. CHURCH

HEROES AND KINGS: Stories from the Greek. Sixth Thousand. Price 1s. 6d., cloth.

'This volume is quite a little triumph of neatness and taste.'—*Saturday Review.*

THE STORIES OF THE ILIAD AND THE ÆNEID. With Illustrations. Seventh Thousand. Price 1s., sewed, or 1s. 6d., cloth.

'The attractive and scholar-like rendering of the story cannot fail, we feel sure, to make it a favourite at home as well as at school.'—*Educational Times.*

THE BURNING OF ROME: A Story of Nero's Days. With Sixteen Illustrations. Price 5s., cloth.

'Is probably the best of the many excellent tales that Mr. Church has produced.'—*Athenæum.*

WITH THE KING AT OXFORD: A Story of the Great Rebellion. With Coloured Illustrations. Fifth Thousand. Price 5s., cloth.

'Excellent sketches of the times.'—*Athenæum.*

A YOUNG MACEDONIAN, in the Army of Alexander the Great. With Coloured Illustrations. Price 5s., cloth.

'The book is full of true classical romance.'—*Spectator.*

THE COUNT OF THE SAXON SHORE: A Tale of the Departure of the Romans from Britain. With Sixteen Illustrations. Third Thousand. Price 5s., cloth.

'"The Count of the Saxon Shore" will be read by multitudes of young readers for the sake of the story, which abounds in moving adventures; older readers will value it for its accurate pictures of the last days of Roman Britain.'—*Spectator.*

THE HAMMER: A Story of the Maccabean Times. By Rev. A. J. CHURCH and RICHMOND SEELEY. With Illustrations. Second Edition. Price 5s., cloth.

'Mr. Alfred Church and Mr. Richmond Seeley have joined their forces in producing a vivid picture of Jewish life and character.'—*Guardian.*

THE GREEK GULLIVER. Stories from Lucian. With Illustrations. New Edition. Price 1s. 6d., cloth. 1s., sewed.

'Every lover of literature must be pleased to have Lucian's good-natured mockery and reckless fancy in such an admirable English dress.'—*Saturday Review.*

ROMAN LIFE IN THE DAYS OF CICERO. With Coloured Illustrations. Sixth Thousand. Price 5s., cloth.

'The best prize book of the season.'—*Journal of Education.*

THE CHANTRY PRIEST OF BARNET: A Tale of the Two Roses. With Coloured Illustrations. Fifth Thousand. Price 5s., cloth.

'This is likely to be a very useful book, as it is certainly very interesting and well got up.'—*Saturday Review.*

TO THE LIONS: A Tale of the Early Christians. With Coloured Illustrations. Fourth Thousand. Price 3s. 6d., cloth.

LONDON : SEELEY & CO., LIMITED, ESSEX ST., STRAND.

PICTURESQUE PLACES

A SERIES OF ILLUSTRATED BOOKS

THE BRITISH SEAS. By W. CLARK RUSSELL, and other Writers. With Sixty Illustrations, after HENRY MOORE, R.A., J. C. HOOK, R.A., COLIN HUNTER, A.R.A., HAMILTON MACALLUM, and other Artists. 6s., cloth.

LANCASHIRE. Brief Historical and Descriptive Notes. By LEO GRINDON. With many Illustrations by A. BRUNET-DEBAINES, H. TOUSSAINT, R. KENT THOMAS, and others. 6s., cloth.

PARIS. In Past and Present Times. By P. G. HAMERTON. With many Illustrations by A. BRUNET-DEBAINES, H. TOUSSAINT, JACOMB HOOD, and others. 6s., cloth.

THE RUINED ABBEYS OF YORKSHIRE. By W. CHAMBERS LEFROY. With many Illustrations by A. BRUNET-DEBAINES and H. TOUSSAINT. 6s., cloth.

OXFORD. Chapters by A. LANG. With many Illustrations by A. BRUNET-DEBAINES, H. TOUSSAINT, and R. KENT THOMAS. 6s., cloth.

CAMBRIDGE. By J. W. CLARK, M.A. With many Illustrations by A. BRUNET-DEBAINES and H. TOUSSAINT. 6s., cloth.

WINDSOR. By W. J. LOFTIE. Dedicated by permission to Her Majesty the Queen. With many Illustrations by HERBERT RAILTON. 6s.

STRATFORD-ON-AVON. In the Middle Ages and the Time of the Shakespeares. By S. L. LEE. With many Illustrations by E. HULL. 6s., cloth.

EDINBURGH. Picturesque Notes. By ROBERT LOUIS STEVENSON. With many Illustrations by W. E. LOCKHART, R.S.A. 3s. 6d., cloth ; 5s., Roxburghe.

CHARING CROSS TO ST. PAUL'S. By JUSTIN M'CARTHY. With Illustrations by JOSEPH PENNELL. 6s., cloth.

A few Copies of the Guinea Edition of some of these volumes, containing the original etchings, can still be had.

LONDON : SEELEY & CO., LIMITED, ESSEX ST., STRAND.

THE PORTFOLIO

ARTISTIC MONOGRAPHS. *Price 2s. 6d. net.*

1894

LONDON   SEELEY & CO., LIMITED, ESSEX ST., STRAND.

THE PORTFOLIO

ARTISTIC MONOGRAPHS. *Price* 2s. 6d. *net.*

MONTHLY.

Each number has about 80 pp. of letterpress, and is complete in itself. The illustrations generally consist of four copper-plates and twenty illustrations in the text.

1895

THE EARLY WORK OF RAPHAEL. By JULIA CARTWRIGHT.

W. Q. ORCHARDSON. By WALTER ARMSTRONG.

CLAUDE LORRAIN. By GEORGE GRAHAME.

WHITEHALL. By W. J. LOFTIE.

JAPANESE WOOD ENGRAVINGS. By WILLIAM ANDERSON.

ANTOINE WATTEAU. By CLAUDE PHILLIPS.

THE ISLE OF WIGHT. By C. J. CORNISH.

RAPHAEL IN ROME. By JULIA CARTWRIGHT.

DUTCH ETCHERS OF THE SEVENTEENTH CENTURY. By LAURENCE BINYON.

WILLIAM BLAKE. By RICHARD GARNETT.

THE RENAISSANCE OF SCULPTURE IN BELGIUM. By O. G. DESTRÉE.

GERARD DAVID, PAINTER AND ILLUMINATOR. By J. W. H. WEALE.

LONDON: SEELEY & CO., LIMITED, ESSEX ST., STRAND.

FAMOUS SCENERY

THE RIVERS OF DEVON. From Source to Sea. By JOHN LL. WARDEN PAGE. With Map, 4 Etchings, and 16 other Illustrations. Crown 8vo, cloth. Price 7s. 6d.

"The book is a capital one to read as a preparation for a tour in Devon, or to take as a companion on the way."—*Scotsman*.

Also a cheap edition, cloth, 3s. 6d.

AN EXPLORATION OF DARTMOOR. By J. LL. W. PAGE. With Map, Etchings, and other Illustrations. Third Edition. Crown 8vo, cloth. Price 7s. 6d.

"Mr. Page is an admirable guide. He takes his readers up hill and down dale, leaving no corner of Dartmoor unexplored. An enthusiastic lover of its rough beauties, he infuses his book and friends with something of his spirited energy."—*Morning Post*.

Also a cheap edition, cloth, 3s. 6d.

AN EXPLORATION OF EXMOOR. By J. LL. W. PAGE. With Map, Etchings, and other Illustrations. Third Edition. Crown 8vo, cloth. Price 7s. 6d.

"Mr. Page has evidently got up his subject with the care that comes of affection, and the result is that he has produced a book full of pleasant reading."—*Graphic*.

THE PEAK OF DERBYSHIRE. By JOHN LEYLAND. With Map, Etchings, and other Illustrations by HERBERT RAILTON and ALFRED DAWSON. Crown 8vo, cloth. Price 7s. 6d.; Roxburghe, 12s. 6d.

"Altogether, Mr. Leyland has produced a delightful book on a delightful subject, and it is impossible to lay it down without regret."—*Saturday Review*.

THE YORKSHIRE COAST AND THE CLEVELAND HILLS AND DALES. By JOHN LEYLAND. With Etchings, Map, and other Illustrations by ALFRED DAWSON and LANCELOT SPEED. Crown 8vo, cloth. Price 7s. 6d.; Roxburghe, 12s. 6d.

"Written with judgment, good taste, and extensive knowledge."—*Spectator*.

"Unique in itself, 'The Yorkshire Coast' should be in the hands of every person who professes interest in the history of Yorkshire."—*Yorkshire Gazette*.

LONDON : SEELEY & CO., LIMITED, ESSEX ST., STRAND.

WORKS BY MRS. MARSHALL

A Series of Historical Stories, with Illustrations.

In Cloth Boards, large crown 8vo., price 5s.

THE MASTER OF THE MUSICIANS. A Story of Handel's Days.

KENSINGTON PALACE: IN THE DAYS OF QUEEN MARY II. Second Edition.

PENSHURST CASTLE: IN THE TIME OF SIR PHILIP SIDNEY. Fourth Thousand.

IN THE SERVICE OF RACHEL, LADY RUSSEL. Fourth Thousand.

WINIFREDE'S JOURNAL. A Story of Exeter and Norwich in the days of Bishop Hall. Fourth Thousand.

WINCHESTER MEADS IN THE DAYS OF BISHOP KEN. Sixth Thousand.

UNDER SALISBURY SPIRE: IN THE DAYS OF GEORGE HERBERT. Ninth Thousand.

IN THE CITY OF FLOWERS. Third Thousand.

ON THE BANKS OF THE OUSE. A Tale of the Times of Newton and Cowper. Fourth Thousand.

IN FOUR REIGNS. The Recollections of ALTHEA ALLINGHAM. Fifth Thousand.

UNDER THE MENDIPS. Sixth Thousand.

IN THE EAST COUNTRY with Sir Thomas Browne, Knight. Fifth Thousand.

IN COLSTON'S DAYS. A Story of Old Bristol. Fifth Thousand.

LIFE'S AFTERMATH. A Story of a Quiet People. With Illustrations. Thirteenth Thousand.

JOANNA'S INHERITANCE. A Story of Young Lives. Fifth Thousand.

DAME ALICIA CHAMBERLAYNE. Memories of Troublous Times. Fourth Thousand.

CONSTANTIA CAREW. An Autobiography.

THE MISTRESS OF TAYNE COURT. Illustrated. Fourth Thousand.

MRS WILLOUGHBY'S OCTAVE. A Tale. Third Thousand.

LONDON : SEELEY & CO., LIMITED, ESSEX ST., STRAND.

990836